The New Pharisee

The New Pharisee

Jeff Saxton

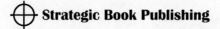
Strategic Book Publishing

Note: All scriptural references are taken the NIV Bible.

Strategic Book Publishing
An imprint of Writers Literary & Publishing Services, Inc.
845 Third Avenue, 6th Floor — #6016
New York, NY 10022
www.StrategicBookPublishing.com

ISBN: 978-1-60693-976-5
SKU: 1-60693-976-9

Printed in the United States of America

This book is dedicated to all of those who have been wounded, abused, persecuted and disillusioned by the New Pharisees throughout the world.

Contents

Prologue

It's AD 31—The Year of Our Lord. A young man from Nazareth is going around the land stirring up the people, calling himself the *Son of God,* doing miracles, breaking the religious rules.

And it makes Nicodemus furious.

After all, Nicodemus is a Pharisee. He is an expert in the Law of Moses and in the oral traditions of the Jewish elders. He studied and applied himself for years to reach this honorable position. The Jews respect him and follow him because he is a religious leader. He represents the God of Abraham, Isaac, and Jacob. He teaches in the synagogues, for heaven's sake! Not only that, but he is even a member of the ruling council! And this Jesus has the nerve to tell everybody that Pharisees are hypocrites.

Nicodemus has made up his mind. This lunatic must be stopped. Somehow. Surely, this Jesus is doing these miracles by the power of Beelzebub. But, Nicodemus continues to listen and

1

watch. He continues to follow from a distance. He can't help but sense the power and authority in Jesus' voice. It's even in his eyes, this mysterious wonder, and absolute confidence in who he claims to be. This man speaks of God as if he has seen Him. Jesus speaks of heaven as a place he has actually been before.

Slowly, surely, inescapably, Nicodemus begins to hang onto every word this man utters. And slowly, surely, and inescapably, the young rabbi begins to make sense. For the first time, Nicodemus begins to see inside himself—the shallowness, the emptiness, the coldness of his religion. He senses the foundation of his spiritual pride and self-preservation is crumbling, with no hope of recovery. His soul is undone. His motives revealed as if opened up before the entire heavenly host. He wants to run and hide from this man and never return. But he can't leave. He can't turn around. Something inside him won't let him.

It's not that Jesus will not let him turn away. But, inside of Nicodemus is a heart that longs to know God, which yearns to escape the dryness and deadness of a soul that has long since departed from the childlike desire to simply know the Almighty and his ways. Perhaps fearing persecution from his peers, he walks the countryside in the moonlight, searching for the dynamic rabbi. On the eve of this wonderful day, Nicodemus finds Jesus. He really wants to know God. But, he has no idea how to get there. Jesus explains, "I tell you the truth, no one can see the kingdom of God unless he is born again."

Nicodemus is confused, initially. But, Jesus has a way of explaining things to those who long to know the Father. And then Jesus says what is now one of the most well known verses in all of Scripture, "For God so loved the world that he gave his one and only Son, that whoever believes in him shall not perish but have eternal life." (John 3:16)

Very likely, Nicodemus left Jesus that evening a new man. At least, he surely had a realization of what it truly meant to be a man or woman of God. We don't really know what happened to him after Jesus died and rose again. Did he leave his position and ministry to follow the way of this Galilean? Did he stay in the sect of the Pharisees and work towards the spiritual renewal of his colleagues? Did he become a follower and go off to other lands preaching the Gospel to the poor? We don't know.

We *do* know that he could no longer live an externally based religious life—justifying himself by performing various spiritual activities. When Jesus comes to us in the core of our hearts, he shows us our bankruptcy. He shows us that, no matter how much we know, or how long we have been Christians, we all live this new life by grace, through faith in what Christ has done on the cross.

We are forever changed when we have believed the Gospel.

WHAT IS THE GOSPEL?

The Gospel is not solely the *message* of faith in Christ. Rather, the Gospel is the good news for those who *repent,* and *believe* the Gospel. (Mark 1:15) Jesus encouraged Nicodemus that whoever believes in Him would not perish. Believing in this sense is more than mental ascent or theological adherence. We are commanded to believe in the sense of commitment to that

which we believe, and in whom we believe. This is where many
"Christians" have problems today. They think that *agreeing* with
the Gospel theologically is the same thing as *believing*. Actually,
many have a problem with *believing* itself.

You're probably familiar with the famous story of Frenchman
Charles Blondin, the great tight rope artist and acrobat of the
nineteenth century. Blondin greeted a huge crowd of fans before
he walked over Niagara Falls in 1859. The crowd began chant-
ing his name at the beginning of the great challenge before him,
"Blondin! Blondin! Blondin!" Blondin turned to the crowd just
before he set his feet on the tightrope and cried out, "Do you
believe that the great Blondin can walk across?" The crowd
shouted louder, "We believe! We believe! We believe!" Blondin
got up on the great tight rope, but before he began the incredibly
long and treacherous walk all the way across the falls, he asked
once again, "Do you believe the great Blondin can walk back
across the falls?" They shouted, "We believe! We believe! We
believe!" And then, something came to Blondin's mind.
Whether this was planned ahead of time is unknown. He put a
wheelbarrow on the tightrope, and then he asked a very strange
question to the crowd, "Which of you truly believes that the
great Blondin can cross the falls? Come now and sit in this
wheelbarrow." The crowd was dumbfounded. No one volunteered to get into the wheelbarrow. Finally, a young man stepped
out from the crowd and said, "I believe." He sat down in the
wheelbarrow as Blondin pushed him across the falls. They
arrived safely on the other side.[1]

Many people claimed to believe that day. But truly, only one *actually* believed in Blondin. The rest merely *claimed* to believe in him.

Jesus has that same desire for sincerity that entered Blondin that day. He would say to you and me, "Which of you truly believe in me? If you believe, lose your life, pick up your cross, and follow me."[2] Believing is about committing to that which we say we believe. There is no faith without commitment. Commitment is a risk, for we do not know what is ahead of us, or what the ramifications of our commitment may mean. Faith without risk is merely a concept, a fantasy notion. It has no actual substance until it risks. It is not enough to be faithful to the *message* of the Gospel. We must be faithful to the *Messiah* of the message. This is the proverbial fork in the road. This is where the true believer parts ways with the others.

Faith without risk is merely a concept, a fantasy notion.

When we give our lives for the Gospel, we then believe the Gospel.

When we believe the Gospel, we judge no man. We speak evil of no other. We have no grounds for spiritual pride. We have no place to seek the respect and honor of other men. We deflect such praise and honor for we know only One is worthy. Our gifts are not our own. He gave them with no help from us. He gave us the understanding to know his Word and his ways. He builds his kingdom by his Spirit. Our ideas are foolish. Even if they bring forth earthly results, this has little, if nothing, to do with heavenly fruit that will remain after trial by fire.

Only this question remains, will you believe, and obey, and be faithful to the Gospel to the end?

The Pharisees of Jesus' day failed. Their pride and ego blinded them from seeing. They were too intoxicated with the perks and pleasures of being religious leaders. This removed a whole generation from the only hope that could save them. When we allow spiritual pride, legalism, and external religious rules to block out the Holy Spirit, we also, in effect, stand against God. We oppose him. We turn him away. We choose to let the people burn and perish. The Pharisee sect of those days may be long gone, but these same characteristics of the Pharisees are alive and well in the world today. Perhaps they are at work in your life. Perhaps you and I are the modern version of the Pharisee in more ways than we would imagine.

This book is an attempt to help you and me to remove this New Pharisee from within us.

INTRODUCING…"CHRISTIAN PHARISEES"

I have been thinking about the concept of the *Christian Pharisee* for several years. I'm not sure when it was that I first considered this term. I have had several opportunities to study the Pharisees in depth as this whole idea has continued to take shape in my thinking—both in personal devotional time as well as in Bible training at a theological institution. Formal study is definitely an advantage in terms of having the time to dig into the biblical material, historical background, and context of the Pharisees of the New Testament. This really helped me develop a solid foundation for understanding who these people were and why Jesus was always finding himself in opposition to them.

Initially, when I was preparing to write this book, I was going to approach it from an academic point of view. I really wanted to dig into the original text and then season this scholarly salad with quotes from all of the biblical scholars and historical experts. But, something changed my mind, although I am thrilled to include some insightful thoughts from some of my favorite authors. It wasn't that I wanted to impress you as you read along, but I did want to give my hypotheses a weightier authority.

I believe God changed my mind as I read the scriptures regarding the Pharisees. You see, I realized that I was not trusting God's Word to do what it can do. It needs no help from any man or woman, no matter how impressive they are. God's Word *is the authority* on this and all other topics! Of course, Bible study aids such as dictionaries, historical and cultural materials, handbooks, and lexicons are a great aid in studying the scriptures in depth. Anyone who has a Bible and a heart for the Lord can grasp the same basic truths that will be sure to revolutionize their views of legalism, hypocrisy, and most importantly, faith in the living Christ.

I write this now with the idea that you can snuggle in your reading chair on a cold or rainy day with your Bible, this book, and a nice hot cup of coffee or cappuccino. But, don't get too comfortable! You may also want to spend a little time on your knees.

A CHALLENGE TO YOU

In the following pages, I want to challenge your faith. At least, I want to challenge you with a proposition: I want to propose to you that the modern-day Pharisee lives and breathes, not within a Jewish synagogue or inside a cultic temple, but in the organized structures of Christianity. This is not to say that everyone involved with organized Christianity is a viper and a whitewashed wall! Nevertheless, many Pharisees exist today in our churches, even in leadership positions. We must work to remove all manner of hypocrisy and legalism within.

As I study the Pharisees, sometimes I see myself in certain areas. I am working to remove the New Pharisee within me. Jesus told the disciples to "be on guard!"[3] In effect, he was saying to them and he says to us now, "Watch out! The same hypocrisy that infiltrated and corrupted the Pharisees is like leaven! Even a hint of it can corrupt you disciples as well!"

I want to propose to you that the modern-day Pharisee lives and breathes, not within a Jewish synagogue or inside a cultic temple, but in the organized structures of Christianity.

The purpose of this book is two-fold: first, to help you see who the New Pharisee really is so that you can be on your guard—watch out for the leaven of the New Pharisee! Secondly, the purpose of this book is to help you locate and eliminate the New Pharisee within YOU.

The New Pharisee is not found in the Jewish religion and culture of today. As you will see, the New Pharisee must be intrinsically attached to and part of the Christian community *by definition*. You will not find the New Pharisee anywhere else. Only within the true, authentic structure of God's established authority here on earth can there be such a person who embodies today everything that the Pharisees embodied then.

Lastly, I warn you with this: after reading this book, you may conclude that you more resemble a Pharisee than a follower of Christ. If so, I most seriously encourage you to repent and then bring forth fruit of that repentance. Perhaps you should repent verbally before the church. If you are part of a small group, (I don't see how you can remove all manner of shallowness and hypocrisy without being part of a small group or accountability group) confess it to the group and have them pray for you.

Also, I am becoming increasingly convinced that hypocrisy can be like any other addiction and must be dealt with in similar ways. Usually there are deep-seeded issues from as far back as childhood that set the tide in motion for covering up hurts and weaknesses. Somewhere early on, the Pharisaical individual began building and maintaining an image that was not, and is not real. People who have built such an image are in store for a difficult journey toward authenticity. I pray you will have the courage and strength to allow Jesus to break you, build you, fill you…and restore you.

1

Identifying the New Pharisee

The state of Christianity in the west has been in stagnation for years. The latest ARIS (American Religious Identification Survey) from 2008 reports an 11% drop in the percentage of Americans who call themselves Christians since the last ARIS survey in 1990.[1] The statistics from the 2000 National Church Surveys by George Barna revealed a decrease of Christian vitality in the lives of its adherents in almost every facet. The number of Christian conversions in North America did not increase in the 1990s as it had on the other continents.[2] And yet, many would most likely declare that things have never been better. The buildings being built, the increase in denominational and individual church budgets, the growing numbers of attendees— these things would (some say *should*) seem to equate growth in Christian living and faith at an individual level.

But the facts prove otherwise. In fact, certain misdeeds such as divorce and pornographic addiction are as prevalent, if not more prevalent, within the church than without. More and more "Christian" youth are having sex with a greater number of partners. Pornography use on the Internet is skyrocketing with Christian men and women...and children. In addition, many other problems beset us inside the church. How many people have experienced rejection, judgment, condemnation, and hypocrisy from within the walls of a church building? Far too many have.

We sing, we build, we strive, and we work. It certainly cannot be said of us in the western church that we are lazy. But with all our labor, what are we producing? Wouldn't any competent businessperson ask that? If Christianity were a business, how would we rate our production? If we were in a board meeting discussing the business of Christianity, we would ask some of the following questions: What is the purpose of this organization? What is it we are trying to produce? To whom are we marketing this product? Are we achieving some level of success? Are we fulfilling our vision—the original vision of our founder?

Looking at the current organizational paradigms in Christianity, one might conclude that we are merely producing financial contributors who fund building programs. Others suggest that we are producing just crowds of admirers to a few super-clergy personalities who perform for us every Sunday morning. Anymore, it seems when you hear someone ask the questions "Is your church growing?" or "Is your ministry growing?" what they are really asking is, "*Is your attendance increasing?*"

Taking a deeper look into the hearts of men and women, we are generally most concerned with appearance, form, and style. We are in danger of becoming more and more like the Israel of old of whom God said, "These people...honor me with their lips. But their hearts are far from me." (Isaiah 29:13)

The biblical model for this kind of hypocritical religiosity found today is most completely defined by a popular religious classification of Jewish leaders two thousand years ago—*The Pharisee!*

THE GOSPEL ACCORDING TO...PHARISEES?

When you think of the word *Pharisee,* what comes to your mind? Some might think of snobby, religious guru-types in white cloaks with big, wrapped turbans on their heads. That seems to be the image portrayed in various films about the life of Jesus Christ over the years. I don't know how accurate it is. You probably know that the Pharisees were Jews, and they were the leaders of the Jewish religion at the time of Christ. After that, it may get a little fuzzy. They were the people with whom Jesus always fought. Most of us know that much.

The Pharisees are mentioned in the four Gospels almost as many times as the twelve disciples. Gaining a basic knowledge of this group of people is vital in understanding the life and ministry of Christ. Dare I say that the Pharisees were the bad guys of the greatest story ever told? I think they were. They were the antagonists. In a blockbuster film, the Pharisee would have been the nemesis—the enemy of the hero. But would they have appeared to be the bad guys at that time and place? It's human nature to point the finger at someone else. It's natural for us to pass the buck or to think everyone else has a problem except us. Let us remember that the Pharisees were all too much like you and me. They were serious. They were sincere and devout. They meant business. They thought they were so right. And…they were dead wrong!

As you might have noticed from the scriptures, Jesus characterized the Pharisees as being completely infected with hypocrisy. After feeding the multitudes with the miracle of the loaves and fishes, Jesus used the symbolism of bread multiplying in Luke 12:2 when he said to his disciples, "Be on your guard against the yeast of the Pharisees, which is hypocrisy." Of course, the disciples had no idea what he was talking about, as usual.

I have a hunch that there were numerous times when the twelve sat by themselves and discussed some of Jesus' eccentricities while he was away praying. I can just hear them saying, "So, do you think he's okay? I mean, maybe he's getting a little sunstroke. My doctor tells me to drink a lot of water and wear plenty of sun block in this torturous, Judean sunlight!" Okay, maybe they didn't know about sun block then. But I am sure they wondered at times if he was in his right mind.

Jesus warned them as he said, "Be careful…Be on your guard against the yeast of the Pharisees and Sadducees!" (Matthew 16:6) After this comment, they really didn't know what to think. Matthew 16:7 records their response, "They discussed this among themselves and said, 'It is because we didn't bring any bread.'"

I find that amusing. There seems to be a slight air of pride in that statement. The disciples sound so sure that they know what he is talking about. I can just hear the disciples—Peter, James and John in particular because they seem like militant vigilantes to me—announcing "Wait Jesus! We know what you are saying. Of course! It's so clear! Watch out because the Pharisees and Sadducees will take all our bread from us. Yes! How clever! How insightful of you, Jesus. It's what we've thought all along. They will conspire with the Romans and together they will not only take all our bread, but the entire country as well if we let them. To arms! To arms!"

They get up and get ready to fight with the Messiah about whom they have always dreamed. And in my imagination, I can see Jesus giving them a gentle, verbal backhand as they sit back down. In verse 8 of Matthew 16 he says, "You of little faith." And he corrects them again!

I don't know about you, but that's usually the way it goes with the Lord and me. That's okay. His corrections are gentle and loving, as long as we don't get so hard-hearted that it takes a really hard backhand.

Jesus wanted the disciples to see something. But he didn't spell it out. He wanted them to perceive it for themselves. If we always must be told what to believe, we will never be able to believe anything for ourselves. Jesus wanted to make the disciples think for themselves. He used parables for this very reason. He knew that smart people who had no faith would not be able to grasp the truths of the kingdom. Socrates used this same method for similar reasons—because it works! Both Socrates and Jesus had the habit of answering questions with other questions.

I recall a time when I was around twelve years old. I really
wanted a brand new racecar set. I begged my father constantly.
He would never give me a straight answer. Finally, I blurted out
one day, "Dad! Why can't I have a racecar set?" My dad replied,
"How long did you play with the train set I bought you last
year?" I couldn't answer because I played with it for maybe two
weeks. I got bored and never even finished setting up the track. I
knew he had me. I couldn't answer.

My dad had not only given me an answer, but he also taught
me a lesson. In fact, I was just as troubled with myself after that
as I was with his answer. For weeks, and even years, I never for-
got that lesson. Even today, whenever I see something I want, I
see my dad sitting in his chair in the living room asking me how
long I had my train set before I became bored with it. Wow!
What a powerful way to teach and to reveal wisdom!

The Pharisees were experts in the Law. Many had probably
memorized the entire Septuagint (the Old Testament in Greek)
and could repeat it verbatim upon request. They were intelligent
and smart. And they never could figure out what Jesus meant in
his parables. I guess we should cut the disciples slack. They
were a little slow in learning the truths of the kingdom of God,
but they were catching on. Jesus continued to challenge them in
their faith.

PHARISEES AND SADDUCEES

Originally, the term Pharisee (first used during the reign of
John Hyrcanus in 135–105 BC) was reserved for that most sincere Jewish sect that was committed to taking the Law literally

and observing it wholeheartedly and completely. Pharisees, "separated unto God,"[3] began as a collection of disenchanted Jews who wanted to separate themselves from the evils that had been spreading in Judea for years. They were successors to the Hasidim, pious Jews who joined the Maccabees in opposing Syrian domination during the years 166–142 BC.[4] To be sure, before and during Christ's earthly life, there were great evils introduced by the Romans: homosexuality, immorality, paganism, imperialistic crimes of various kinds including confiscation of property, forced military participation, and other lewd and cruel acts. The Romans were known for their brutality and vileness. This created an arousal of no small amount of righteous indignation in the hearts of the Jews.

One can hardly blame them. The city of Jerusalem was a sacred place—the location of the temple and the Holy of Holies. For centuries, the Jews were awaiting the coming of Messiah. He would strike down the Gentile trespassers and deliver Israel from the Roman occupation. The Gentiles were seen as an unclean race; unfit for salvation. Around AD 40, God would show Peter through a dream[5] that the Gentiles were clean; they had been accepted as potential children of God, depending on their willingness to obey the Gospel of Christ.

The Sadducees, also a religious sect of Judaism, were very similar to the Pharisees in that they were moral and devout and had a measure of authority within the ranks of the Jewish faith. Together with the chief priests and elders, they joined forces with the highly feared and respected Jewish council called the Sanhedrin, and eventually arranged the arrest and crucifixion of

Christ in *Anno Domini* (year of our Lord) 33. The Pharisees became the leading sect of the Jewish authorities after that time.[6]

The Pharisees were moral. They were conservative. They stood for moral purity and righteousness. But what started out as a holy passion to obey the Law of Moses (the Torah), ended up being an obsessive legalistic craze of strict adherence to the oral traditions of the elders. Somewhere along the line, hypocrisy crept in until they reached the stage where Jesus described them as a "brood of vipers." (Matthew 3:7)

How could this happen? Where did they go wrong? Or could it be that they were wrong from the beginning?

A STORY FROM BIBLE COLLEGE

I had the joy and privilege of attending a Bible college after graduating from high school. The joke at every Christian college is that the girls are there to get their MRS. degree (marriage degree). Bible colleges are similarly called *bridal colleges* by many of these same marriage-seeking individuals. I have to admit that I was thinking the same thing but just acted cool about it. You know what I mean? The cool type—they're the kind that walk down the hallway pretending not to notice an attractive member of the opposite sex. And as the two apparently uninterested parties pass each other like ships in the night, they turn back when they think the other is not looking to get another glimpse of each other.

Many meet their mates in college. But when the eager spouse-seeker finally meets and marries *the one,* there are sometimes not necessarily letdowns, but certain adjustments in expectations.

Let's face it, we can't all marry Miss America or Mr. Olympia. It's one thing to look forward in expectation to a certain thing or person. But many times, we have to adjust our expectations when "faith" and "waiting" become "sight" and "arrival."

I think you can see the disciples, and everyone else, going through this same thing with Jesus Christ. After thousands of years of waiting, it is understandable that the Jews developed expectations of who their deliverer would be, what he would look like, and what he would accomplish. The Messiah became the most looked for and awaited figure of the Jewish faith. Indeed today, the Jews still look for the Messiah. They have rejected Jesus Christ because he did not fulfill certain expectations.

UNDERSTANDING THE PHARISEE

To understand the New Pharisee, which as I have stated may be within us, we must understand the Pharisee of Jesus' day. It only made sense to the Pharisees that the Messiah would deliver them from the Roman forces and set up a Jewish rule unprecedented even in Solomon's day. What about all those prophesies concerning a new Jerusalem and God's reigning over the earth from Zion? Can we blame them for thinking that the Messiah would set up God's reign in a visible, tangible kingdom upon the earth in their lifetime?

Sure, we look today with hindsight and can easily see that they were wrong about the Messiah coming to reign in Jerusalem back then. It's 2,000 years later, and he still isn't reigning physically in Jerusalem. But what would we have thought back then? Would we have understood the Messiah to be a lamb who was slain from the foundation of the world? Would we have looked in expectation for a child to be born in a humble place, in a humble town, in such humble circumstances? Would we have traveled afar to follow the star? I guess the only way to answer that is to ask ourselves what we seek presently in our time.

Are we looking with anticipation for Christ's return? Or, are we happy and content with a comfortable life here on earth and lukewarmness in our hearts toward the things of God? Do we seek daily to carry our cross and to fight the good fight of faith? Or are we too busy enjoying life with our spouse and our children? Do we seek to win the lost and reach the world for Christ? Or do we enjoy the nice, safe Christian clique we have found at church and seek to keep it to ourselves? Do we pray and seek the kingdom that is to come? Or are we consumed with increasing our income level, and financial and social status, even our spiritual status?

The answer to those questions will probably answer fairly accurately what kind of Messiah you would have been looking for in first century Palestine.

I know, I know. It is much more desirable to make the Pharisees seem a bit monstrous. We'd rather keep the bad guys far removed from us. We do this all the time in our culture. We slap a label on somebody, and we deceive ourselves into thinking certain people are so much worse than we are. Indeed, others may have done terrible things that we will never do. But we tend to demonize and dehumanize certain people such as murderers, child abusers, those of other creeds, races, cultures, and political persuasions. It feels so much safer, doesn't it? We feel better about ourselves when we dehumanize someone else whom we see as a bad person. It's human nature, I suppose.

This happens all the time when nations go to war. Unfortunately, you can't fire up a nation, and especially your soldiers, with statements like, "Okay soldiers! Get out there and shoot as many enemy targets as you possibly can with this one thought in mind: They are all scared young teenagers just like you!" No. Wars are better fought by dehumanizing and demonizing the enemy. How often do we do that with people we know to be sinners, or perceive to be evil? We know that horrible acts are committed on both sides in war. At the end of the day, the people we are most afraid of are not that different than we are.

SOME PHARISEES REPENTED

This is helpful in understanding the Pharisees. They weren't all bad guys. Nicodemus was a Pharisee—and a seeker of the truth. After all, we have probably the most well known verse in the Bible because of Nicodemus. John 3:16 says, "For God so loved the world that He gave His one and only Son, that whoever believes in Him shall not perish but have eternal life." Nicodemus sincerely and humbly inquired of Jesus how he might get to heaven. We also learn about the need to be born again because of Nicodemus. He may very well have become a follower of Christ after that night.

Places of spiritual authority tend to attract the best and the worst, sort of like running for a political office. The folks who truly want to seek the Lord, serve him, and help others find him, will be attracted to spiritual authority positions for all of the right reasons. Yet, those who want to gain glory, honor, and the other fringe benefits of leadership will be attracted to spiritual authority positions for all of the wrong reasons. One might retort, "Yeah, but spiritual authority can be a real headache. Whoever wants that role can have it!" True. Being in a place of spiritual authority can be painful and challenging, if it is carried out correctly.

Nicodemus strikes me as a man who really wanted to honor God in his role as a Pharisee. We read the same about Paul in Philippians 3:5. He was a Hebrew of Hebrews, and a Pharisee. Paul sincerely believed he was helping God (doing God a favor) by arresting and killing the disciples that followed the ways of the crazy man from Nazareth. Both Nicodemus and Paul represent men who were very devout and very sincere. Don't you think that sounds like two wonderful characteristics for a man of the cloth to have? However, Jesus had something altogether different to say about the devout and sincere Pharisees.

THE PHARISEES ACCORDING TO JESUS

The denunciations of the Pharisees by Jesus are devastating! Matthew 23 records the lengthiest denunciation of the Pharisees in the Bible. Imagine being called any of the following names: blind guides, hypocrites, brood of vipers, sons of hell, whitewashed tombs, fools, snakes, etc. You would definitely have had the feeling that Jesus was a little upset at you. The Pharisees were thoroughly condemned by Christ. There could not possibly be a more severe judgment than what Jesus laid down.[7]

In my junior high school, we had a principal who was most feared by the students. Dr. Eugene Young had a jet black, bouffant hairdo, and a huge face. He looked like he could have been a bodyguard for some mafia kingpin. He had charisma and charm, but one sure didn't want to get in trouble with him because he could really deliver the thunder. Doc Young always assumed absolute control over a rebellious teen. Some teachers and adults can be intimidated. The six-foot-three, three hundred pound plus Doctor Young was not one of those.

For some reason, I think of Doc Young when I think of the stance that Christ took with these Pharisees. Jesus was not intimidated by the Pharisees. He knew they would certainly plot to arrest him and kill him after this, but he didn't back down. Jesus pulled back the shades, so to speak, and let everyone in on the light of the situation. John chapter eight records a lengthy discussion between Jesus and the Pharisees. At one point, Jesus replied in verse forty-four, "You belong to your father, the devil, and you want to carry out your father's desire."

When the Creator of the universe calls you a son of the devil, you've got problems!

This is not the kind of thing one would say at a political rally. And it certainly is not something one says to a group of people of whom you are afraid. Jesus told them the truth—the horrible, chilling reality of what they had become. When the Creator of the universe calls you a son of the devil, you've got problems!

THE NEW PHARISEE IS A CHRISTIAN!

I use the term Christian in the broadest sense. In other words, any person who *claims* to follow Jesus, I will call a Christian here for the sake of clarity. Today's Pharisee is found within the Christian community. Here are some of the characteristics of the Pharisee of Jesus' day that have direct application to the New Pharisee:

1. They held to orthodox beliefs.

    They believed in heaven and hell. They believed in angels and demons, resurrection of the dead, reward, and retribution after death, and the immortality of the soul.

2. They believed that all human beings were equal in God's sight.

3. They held to a balanced view of the free will of man and God's sovereignty.

4. They had a strong sense of ethics, personal character, and integrity.

5. They sat in the seat of God's ordained authority.[8]

    The Pharisees were in God's ordained position of authority at the time.[9] In fact, Jesus and the disciples taught in the synagogues and temple. They were obviously all Jews, as were the people who attended their teachings. One of the major reasons for Jesus' righteous indignation concerning the Pharisees was this very fact that they "sat in Moses' seat." (Matthew 23:2)

…the New Pharisee many times occupies a position of spiritual authority within the structure of the church leadership, be that in a church or a parachurch ministry.

These factors would indicate that a Pharisee in today's society would also sit in God's ordained seat of authority. This seat of authority today is in Christ, of course. All Christians have been given the authority of Christ. "All authority in heaven and on earth has been given to me." (Matthew 28:18) Indeed, the New Pharisee sits in the place of God's authority. In fact, the New Pharisee many times occupies a position of spiritual authority within the structure of the church leadership, be that in a church or a parachurch ministry.

2

Christian Pharisees

The proposition sounds crazy, doesn't it? How can someone be a Christian and a *son of the devil* at the same time? Well, ultimately you can't be both. As we saw with Nicodemus the Pharisee, some people may have the title of "Christian" or "Pharisee," but God can see past titles. He sees the heart. The point of this proposition is to show us that titles do not have anything to do with our spiritual standing before God. Using the title "Christian" doesn't mean anything.

Hitler called himself a Christian. Many false prophets call themselves Christians. Granted, some of them just skip the middleman and say, "I am Christ." Consider some of the wicked things done in the name of Christ over the centuries: The Crusades, which were acts of militant imperialism carried out in the name of Christ, the various occupations of other countries by Christian nations, and Christians being burned at the stake by other so-called Christians. In our own nation, we have seen people do all manner of evil in the name of Christ. The world isn't fooled. They know that titles mean nothing.

Our first biblical introduction with these interesting people called Pharisees is found in Matthew 3:7–9. Before they gave our Lord so much trouble, they were giving John the Baptist some headaches. John declared, "You brood of vipers! (That must have been a common denunciation back then.) Who warned you to flee from the coming wrath? Produce fruit in keeping with repentance. And do not think you can say to yourselves, 'We have Abraham as our father.' I tell you that out of these stones God can raise up children for Abraham."

Back then, the Pharisees were placing their faith in the fact that they were children of Abraham, which is another way of saying that they were God's people.[1] They were using a title to justify their standing before God. Today, people rest in the fact that they are Christians even though they may show no fruit of their repentance. They have been taught that if they just tell God they are sorry for their sins, they will go to heaven. They are given assurance of their salvation based on an admission to a few doctrinal truths.

THE PHARISEE'S DOCTRINE OF "ASSURANCE"

Let me say right from the start that I believe in the doctrine of assurance by faith. A problem arises, however, when we want to go around giving everybody assurance of his salvation because we may believe a certain doctrine very strongly. There is nothing wrong with teaching the doctrine of assurance of our salvation. What is wrong and completely unscriptural is to give people automatic assurance just because they said a prayer. It reduces the most wonderful moment in this life to a simple pop quiz. It smacks of a groom and bride making vows of faithfulness on their wedding day when all the while they are planning a big group orgy for their honeymoon. If a sane pastor knew their vows were meaningless, he would not marry them in good faith. He would not assure them that God receives their vows. He *may* assure them that God is *offended* with their vows.

We have been teaching people in churches for years now that if they said the sinner's prayer, or agreed with four or five spiritual truths, they could be assured of their salvation. I am not saying that people who pray the sinner's prayer or concur with the basic precepts of the Gospel are not saved. But I *am* saying that it is the Holy Spirit who saves a person and the Holy Spirit who truly knows the heart of the person who appears to have repented. I have prayed the sinner's prayer with many people, and will continue to do so. Do I think those people I prayed with became born again after we prayed? Yes. Am I *certain beyond the shadow of a doubt* that they were born again after we prayed? No. Ultimately, only God knows.

Maybe we have seen people who have repented *and shown fruit* of that repentance suddenly fall under attacks of condemnation of the enemy. To those people, I would say, "Be joyful! He who repents *from the heart* is completely assured of his salvation and God will never take that away from a true child of God!" The fearful new believer might respond, "But then how do I know if I am a child of God? I don't feel like a child of God right now!" I always answer, "Don't go by your feelings. You can't trust feelings. You must have faith in God and what his word promises. If you sincerely repented and you meant that confession of faith in Christ from your heart, God promises you in his Word that you are his child and a new creation! Praise the Lord that your name is written in the book of life and angels are throwing one big party in your name right now!"

There are those prodigal sons and daughters who are truly saved, and yet are not seeking Christ as they first did. But prodigals usually have much sorrow about their sinful lifestyle choices. If they have not truly been born again, they may well be New Pharisees going out and doing all manner of vile wickedness, yet still claiming to be Christians.

There is a difference between the prodigal and the deceived. The difference is the prodigal knows the Father. I have known a number of prodigals. They usually show several evidences of being born of the Spirit even in the midst of their backsliding. I have known a few prodigals that eventually got so cold, I wondered if they had ever really, truly been saved. Perhaps they had not. But this latter kind—the kind that got *fire insurance* so that they could live however they pleased—I doubt they ever were born again. They were possibly converted to a set of Christian ideals, but never converted from death to life by the Spirit of the Living God.

There is a difference between the prodigal and the deceived.

HOW CAN WE KNOW?

We can't know the heart. We should always give people the benefit of the doubt. Jesus explained this principle in the parable of the wheat and the tares. Matthew 13:27–30: "The owner's servants came to him and said, 'Sir, didn't you sow good seed in your field? Where then did the weeds come from?' 'An enemy did this,' he replied. The servants asked him, 'Do you want us to go and pull them up?' 'No,' he answered, 'because while you are pulling the weeds, you may root up the wheat with them. Let both grow together until the harvest.'"

I think this is the best advice regarding assurance. We cannot know the heart of another person. If a person confesses to be a Christian and yet shows little evidence of their faith, it is best to pray for him or talk with him as God leads instead of condemning him. We may pull out a grain of wheat that we thought was a weed.

The New Pharisee has said the prayer and has the proper title.

What we *must not* do is to promise people that they can enter the kingdom of God with a wicked or a clean heart, as long as they say a prayer and repeat some truths back to us. I think we are guilty of teaching *false assurance* at that point. We must warn people that titles mean nothing; prayers mean nothing, and promises mean nothing if they are not sincerely from the heart and true to a person's motives and inner desires. The New Pharisee has said the prayer and has the proper title. He or she would say, "I am a Christian."[2]

One of the most troubling passages of scripture in the four Gospels is found in Matthew 7:21. Jesus said, "Not everyone who says to me, 'Lord, Lord,' will enter the kingdom of heaven, but only he who does the will of my Father who is in heaven. Many will say to me on that day, 'Lord, Lord, did we not prophesy in your name, and in your name drive out demons and perform many miracles?' Then I will tell them plainly, 'I never knew you. Away from me, you evildoers!'"

The Greek word for evildoers is actually better translated lawless ones, having no accountability to God or to the lordship of Christ. You may have grown up in a Christian home. But to quote the late Keith Green, "Going to church doesn't make you a Christian anymore than going into a McDonalds makes you a hamburger."[3] You must be born again!

Being born again does *not* happen *until* the Holy Spirit comes inside and sees the humble sincere heart of faith, bears witness with that person's spirit, and indwells that person, producing fruit of his repentance. This is really what John was saying to the Pharisees: "Don't rest on your background! Don't rest on your title (be it Pharisee or Christian)! Rest on the fact that you are bearing fruit of your repentance!"

This is precisely what Jesus was warning Nicodemus about when He explained, "You must be born again." John Darby, predecessor of Charles Spurgeon, makes the following observation about this late-night meeting between Nicodemus and Jesus in his *Synopsis of the New Testament:*

His conscience was reached. Seeing Jesus, and hearing His testimony, had produced a sense of need in his heart. It is not the knowledge of grace, but it is with respect to man's condition a total change. He knows nothing of the truth, but he has seen that it is in Jesus, and he desires it. He has also at once an instinctive sense that the world will be against him; and he comes by night. The heart fears the world as soon as it has to do with God, for the world is opposed to Him. The friendship of the world is enmity against God. This sense of need made the difference in the case of Nicodemus. He had been convinced like the others. Accordingly, he says, "We know that thou art a teacher come from God." And the source of this conviction was the miracles. But Jesus stops him short; and that because of the true need felt in the heart of Nicodemus. The work of blessing was not to be wrought by teaching the old man. Man needed to be renewed in the source of his nature, without which he could not see the kingdom.[4]

Jesus doesn't lie. Nor does he mislead. The requirements for entering heaven have not changed. Unless you and I have been born again, we cannot enter the kingdom. Yes, *entering the kingdom* also refers to the daily walk of Christians. But how can someone fail to enter the kingdom in terms of lifestyle, and still enter the kingdom in the ultimate sense of going to eternal paradise? They are the proverbial two sides of the same coin.

REPENTANCE AND LORDSHIP

Many people today call themselves Christians, but do not live like Christ. They may be born again and are severely backslidden. Or, they may never have been born of the Spirit of God. But, those who claim to be Christians are telling God, themselves, and everyone else that they have decided to take up their cross and follow Christ. Matthew 10:38 says, "And anyone who does not take his cross and follow me is not worthy of me." Being a Christian has everything to do with following Christ and his lordship. We decided to make Jesus Lord when we were first saved. We must continue to live that out as we go along in our Christian life. Some people will say that we should not tell people that they have to make Jesus Lord in order to repent because that is works. They tend to imply that people can make Jesus their Savior, but they don't have to make him Lord. The reason this is crazy is because repentance is, in itself, an act of lordship. You are repenting of not letting Jesus be Lord of your life…if it is indeed true repentance!

After all, didn't Jesus say that the greatest commandment was to love the Lord your God with *all* your heart, soul, mind, and strength? I don't get the sense of *option* in Jesus' statement here! He says it is the greatest *commandment.* (Matthew 22:37) Surely, the greatest commandment is applicable to new believers as well as to seasoned veterans of the faith. Matter of fact, this command is applicable to all people, both saved and unsaved! You cannot ask Jesus to forgive you of your sins and then not show any fruit of repentance, because if that is your heart, then the Holy Spirit did not draw you in the first place.

Jesus was willing to turn away the crowd by his challenging words of commitment and dedication.

Maybe we should stop trying to shove everyone into heaven. Maybe we should start talking people out of becoming Christians. Jesus was willing to turn away the crowd by his challenging words of commitment and dedication. We must be faithful to all of his teachings, not just the salvation message that we have passed on traditionally as if it was a doctrine of the faith. In actuality, the whole idea of making Jesus one's personal savior was a creation of twentieth century mass evangelism. I am not saying I am against the idea of making the Gospel easy to understand and even praying with someone to receive Christ. But I am saying that avoiding lordship as the Bible defines it—a heart attitude—is not only at best irresponsible, it is hypocritical, and at worst, even heretical.

C. S. Lewis explains, "That is why He (Jesus) warned people to 'count the cost' before becoming Christians. 'Make no mistake' He says, 'if you let me, I will make you perfect. The moment you put yourself in my hands, that is what you are in for. Nothing less, or other, than that.'"[5]

You cannot follow Christ without Him being your Lord. How can we sing out to him that he is our Master, King, Lord, God, Leader, and Ultimate Love if he is not?

I agree that we must not expect new believers to be at the same level of *discipleship* that we are. But they sure should have the same level of *commitment.** Otherwise, how can they receive the Spirit who will not dwell in the heart of someone who lives a life of disobedience? If you disobey God on a constant basis, the Spirit will be quenched. And if you don't even

have a heart of obedience, perhaps He has not come into your
heart at all.

Perhaps this has created more New Pharisees than we could
imagine.

*We will forever remember the confession of the teenage
Christians who did not deny their faith in God and Christ as the
Columbine High School murderers pointed their guns in these
young believer's faces. They proclaimed their faith to the world,
not loving their lives to the death. And then the guns blew them
into eternity. Does anyone question that even the most mature
disciples of God throughout the ages would have at least struggled to give their lives in this same fashion? These teens could
have easily denied their faith and said, "No. I do not believe in
God." If they were able to give their very lives for their Lord, we
should be encouraged to ask the same of others today. I am
embarrassed of the times when I held back on this same kind
of challenge to other young people and seekers of the truth!

I have made a shift in my personal witness and ministry: I am
more often trying to get unsaved people to count the cost before
becoming a Christian. Salvation is free, but discipleship will cost
you everything. You can be saved and be a poor disciple; you could
possibly even be a deserter, for did not even the twelve disciples
desert Christ just before his crucifixion? If you do not consider
yourself a disciple of Christ, it could be that you never did receive
Christ. People that actually have chosen to receive Christ have then
also chosen to become his disciple. And let's drop the semantics;
the moment of your salvation *was* the moment of your discipleship.

IS OBEDIENCE "WORKS?"

In *Moses: A Man of Selfless Dedication,* author and pastor
Chuck Swindoll offered these thoughts concerning lordship:

I am deeply concerned over the shallowness of our spiritual walk in the American church today. Spiritual depth is rare in these landmark days at the turn of a millennium. Our time with God might as well depend on a flip of the coin—heads I do, tails I don't. If I feel like it, great. If I don't, well, He's a God of grace; He understands. Frankly, I do not find such accommodating nonsense in Scripture... God is holy. Exalted. He is the only wise God, the Creator, the Maker, and the sovereign Lord. He is the Master. He tells me what to do, and I have no safe option but to do it. There is no alternative, no multiple choice. We have but one directive, and that is to do his will...Today He's our pal, our understanding buddy, our everlasting bellboy. No, He's not! The Lord is our God.[6]

Because God is, we must do his will. The definition of sin is to choose not to obey him.

People who are truly born again have the desire to follow Christ—

Deitrich Bohnhoeffer asserts, "The only man who has the right to say that he is justified by grace alone is the man who has left all to follow Christ. Such a man knows that the call to discipleship is a gift of grace, and that the call is inseparable from the grace. But those who try to use this grace as a dispensation from following Christ are simply deceiving themselves."[7]

This may sound like *works* to you. But I would submit that only those *not* born of the Spirit would follow Christ out of a works motif. People who are truly born again have the desire to follow Christ—making it an overflow of grace, not a struggle of works. A truly born again Christian has the Spirit residing within him. It is this power that takes what was once impossible to do (works) and transforms it into a walk of grace through faith, where good deeds follow—and the fruit of the spirit naturally grows—effortlessly. An apple tree does not *work* to grow apples. The apples grow *automatically,* with no effort from the tree because of the natural power within the tree to produce apples. In fact, it would be more work for the tree to cease from producing fruit.

It is actually more work for a truly born again believer to *cease* works, than to *do* them. And that sounds like the only true *grace* to me—God's grace gives us the grace naturally to produce good works like a fruit tree. When we fall short, or when we sin, that same grace to do good works is there to renew us, forgive us, wipe the slate clean, pick us up, and hold us as our Father whispers the words "I love you, My child" in our spirits. Then he sends us out to continue the grace of good works. This is the kind of grace that Bonheoffer wanted to see his fellow Lutherans embrace.

If people claim to have been saved and yet also claim that following Christ is works to them, we must take them once again to the cross to see whether they have truly been born of the Spirit. If they indeed have been born again of the Spirit and the Holy Spirit has taken up residence within them, they already have the power to follow, and the only true work involved would be in quenching and stopping the natural works of faith and grace that the Holy Spirit births from within them. (James 2:22)

ONE MORE THING...BAPTISM

In our culture, water baptism is viewed very differently than it was in New Testament times. Even in Christian denominations,

there is a wide variety of opinions on the applicability and importance of water baptism. But, about this one thing we cannot
argue: John the Baptist, Jesus, and the apostles baptized people
immediately following their confessions of faith in Christ. (Mark
16:16; Acts 8:36; 16:33) In the New Testament times, it was
assumed that a new convert was a disciple to that which they had
converted. Water baptism, then, was a symbol and a proclamation
to the whole earth that they had committed their lives to this new
faith or creed. It was part of the salvation experience. Water baptism was the initial declaration of discipleship.

Today, water baptism is not seen as a mandatory event at the
moment of conversion in many countries and cultures. I realize
that there are numerous difficulties in churches and families when
water baptism is misunderstood, or viewed from a traditional doctrine passed down through centuries. I know various denominations have different interpretations regarding baptism. I also
realize that baptism immediately following conversion is not
always possible—the thief on the cross certainly could not get
down from the cross to be baptized, yet Christ called him a justified man as they died there together. But there are many opportunities to baptize new believers. We must seize those
opportunities. Perhaps a return to the practice of water baptism
would also reduce the trend towards New Pharisaism.

LORDSHIP IS A MATTER OF THE HEART

When someone is truly born again, a spiritual miracle has
taken place by the Holy Spirit within his or her spirit. Repentance is the transaction that has taken place. Lordship is simply

the attitude of the heart that has allowed it to take place. In fact, the *attitude of lordship* takes place *before someone repents!* The moment of salvation looks something like this:

Attitude of Lordship + Repent of Self-rule + Request for Forgiveness = Jesus Takes Up Residence

The equation doesn't always look this clear. There is no formula per se. But, these major Holy Spirit transactions usually take place when one is born again. After the moment of being born again, the fruits of repentance will come forth. Again, understand that Lordship does *not* mean perfection or having our spiritual ducks in a row. In essence, it is simply an act of humbling one's self before an almighty, all-powerful God.

Lordship does *not* mean perfection or having our spiritual ducks in a row.

Lordship is an attitude of humility. If anything, repentance *is* works because it is all about turning around in the opposite direction and obeying. Those who say, "You don't have to make Jesus Lord in order to be saved" probably *mean,* "You don't have to *be perfect* in order to be saved," in which case, they are correct. But their statement as defined is incorrect.

Lordship is a heart attitude. It is not a state of perfection.

Plain and simple, one cannot repent without making Jesus Lord of his or her life. Some fight against the lordship doctrine because they misunderstand it. Perhaps they misunderstand it because of the New Pharisee interpretation. You see, the New Pharisee *does* think he or she can attain or has attained a state of sinlessness. I think those who propose that they have every area of their life under the complete control of the Spirit at all times are (1) deceived, (2) proud, (3) ignorant of their own hearts, and (4) ignorant of the plain declarations of scripture regarding our hearts.

Our hearts are wicked above all else! In fact, as one progresses along in the Christian life, he or she is aware of how many areas are *not* under the control of the Spirit as they should be. Lordship does *not mean perfection!* The New Pharisee is the one deceived into thinking he or she is without sin!

Lordship has nothing to do with perfection. Lordship has everything to do with a person's heart desire to follow Christ. Lordship is worked out on a day-to-day basis. True, born again believers can live months, even years, in a backslidden state, not following the lordship of Christ in their lives, and retain their salvation. However, they are in danger, and should be warned that Satan seeks to devour them.

The New Pharisee would possibly even promote lordship. But they themselves would not lift a finger in areas such as mercy, compassion, and acts of selflessness. The Pharisees of Jesus' day believed they were sinless. They believed they had attained perfect lordship. They accused everyone else because of their sins (Matthew 9:10–11), and Christ condemned them. What an indictment!

Thomas Merton asks in *Passion For Peace,* "What is the meaning of a concept (of Christianity) that excludes love, considers it irrelevant, and destroys our capacity to love other human beings, to respond to their needs and their sufferings, to recognize them also as persons, to apprehend their pain as one's own?"[8]

REPENT *AND* BELIEVE THE GOSPEL!

We must promote lordship (as defined above) as Christians. We must not be guilty of creating more New Pharisees. Neither must we create dead, religious-oriented churchgoers. If we do not promote the heart attitude of lordship with those to whom we preach the Gospel, we will continue to create spiritual still-borns—those who have enough truth to be brought near to the kingdom, but never really connect with the Father. We may have prayed the sinner's prayer with them. But, that is not a guarantee. There are those who know they must forsake their sin and follow Jesus because of an understanding of whom they are and who God is. But then there are the spiritual stillborns, those who do not obey the Gospel, although they consider themselves Christians because they prayed the prayer. Some of these seem to be just looking for eternal fire insurance.

It's better for someone to calculate the cost before taking on the name of Christ, than to convert to that which they really do not understand.

Again, it's as if they had a lottery ticket to heaven. They figure, well, I got in. Lucky me. I have no idea what I did, or what it meant, but I'm just glad somebody said I was okay, and that I would never have to worry about going to hell again. Whew!

What a relief. Well, I think I'll go off today and do some more pleasure seeking.

Wisdom would say to take care of proper teaching and instruction on the front end. It's better for someone to calculate the cost before taking on the name of Christ, than to convert to that which they really do not understand. (Luke 14:28-34) Jesus asked people to count the cost. His message was a message of repentance—just like John the Baptist, the prophets, Moses, and anyone else who has any kind of heart for God.

As Walter A. Henrichsen points out in *Disciples Are Made Not Born,* lordship may mean that God will ask us to do some things we do not wish to do.

> Nobody likes the cross. Nobody likes to die. Nobody likes to deny himself. But this is what lordship is all about. A disciple is a disciplined one. He is one who says no to what he wants in deference to what his Lord wants. This disciple does not pamper himself by satisfying his wants and desires in a self-gratifying fashion. When Jesus Christ is lord of your life, every area is under his jurisdiction—your thoughts, your actions, your plans, your vocation, your leisure time, and your life goal. All of these are under His Lordship.[9]

We need to be careful. Jesus condemned the Pharisees. But he did not condemn sinners. I don't think it is our job to condemn anyone. For the rest of our lives, the Father will be perfecting us, revealing areas inside of us that are not under the Spirit's control. This is what is known as the process of sanctification. I say again, sanctification is a process. Coming under the lordship of Christ in every area of our lives is a process. Having the heart of obedience is not a process, but a command for every waking moment of our lives. When we fail, He is faithful to forgive us and to start again. I don't think we should try too hard to judge whether someone is saved or not. It's best to let wheat and tares grow together. You don't want to uproot wheat when you thought it might be a tare. On the other hand, let us confront the New Pharisee whenever we find him—in others and especially in ourselves.

3

The Shift toward Hypocrisy

The New Pharisee is just like the old—he or she is wrapped up in hypocrisy. Hypocrisy takes on many forms, but the essence is still the same. The definition of hypocrisy according to Webster's Dictionary is "a stage actor, a pretender, a person who pretends to be what he is not."[1] It refers to a performer up in front of an audience, perhaps wearing a mask. It may be unfair for unsaved people to condemn the church because of the hypocrites. I mean, you have to admit the world is full of hypocrites also. Be it fair or unfair, we who call ourselves Christians are supposed to be following a man who never wore a mask, never lied, deceived, or manipulated to get his own way. If we name the name of Christ, we are therefore telling people that we have decided to be honest, forthright, vulnerable, and authentic.

The world has every right to expect us to be different. They are the ones who are spiritually bankrupt, not us! (I hope!) In his monumental book, *Mere Christianity,* C. S. Lewis said, "The outer world is quite right to judge Christianity by its results. Christ tells us to judge by results. A tree is known by its fruit; or, as we say, the proof of the pudding is in the eating. When we Christians behave badly, or fail to behave well, we are making Christianity unbelievable to the outside world."[2]

In Jesus' day, the term hypocrite (*hypokrites*) was used very rarely. In fact, Jesus was one of the few to identify another person with this term.[3] Occasions of hypocrisy happen throughout the scriptures. As I mentioned earlier, Jesus warned his disciples to beware of the yeast of the Pharisees, which was hypocrisy.

Yeast is amazing, isn't it? Have you ever baked homemade bread before? Not only do you knead the dough, but also at one point, you add a moderate sprinkling of yeast. It's true! A little yeast leavens the whole lump. It's like a chemical mixture. Add one chemical and you change the entire makeup of the mixture. Another substance that is similar to yeast is seasoning. My father hates oregano. If he smells even a hint of oregano, he will not eat whatever it is my mother has prepared. Obviously, Italian foods use oregano in almost everything. Just a pinch will change the taste of the dish.

Jesus is saying that hypocrisy is the same way. Just a little hypocrisy will infect the whole system, group, or soul of the individual person. It cannot be tolerated! It must be seen as deadly to the survival of the Spirit of Christ in that group or person! Beware of hypocrisy!

In Matthew 23:25–28, probably the most severe exposé takes place against the Pharisees. Jesus declares:

Woe to you, teachers of the law and Pharisees, you hypocrites! You clean the outside of the cup and dish, but inside you
are full of greed and self-indulgence. Blind Pharisee! First clean
the inside of the cup and dish, and then the outside will be clean.
Woe to you, teachers of the law and Pharisees, you hypocrites!
You are like whitewashed tombs, which look beautiful on the
outside, but on the inside are full of dead men's bones and
everything unclean. In the same way, on the outside you appear
to people as righteous but on the inside, you are full of hypocrisy and wickedness.

You can't judge a book by its cover! You've probably heard
that saying a thousand times. But somehow, we forget to apply
this cliché when it comes to religious externalism. Hypocrisy
in spiritual terms is highlighted by this propensity to make
one's self appear holy on the outside, while the inside is
ignored. Such attempts at outward holiness are futile. It is
much like trying to remove a peach tree by plucking off all the
peaches. Sooner or later, that peach tree will bear more
peaches. In order to kill that peach tree, it must be removed
and destroyed at the roots.

Sin will not be stopped or even slowed by outward attempts.

The same is true with the human soul. Sin is birthed from
within a man. Much of Jesus' teaching on sin in the Gospels
speaks to this inner condition. I wonder how much of the sanctification teaching in our churches would change if we were to
rediscover this most basic principle. Sin will not be stopped or

even slowed by outward attempts. Sin can only be stopped by the power of the Spirit of God as he indwells the believer; however, the Holy Spirit must be continually yielded to on a day-to-day basis for this fact to be a daily, living reality. The New Pharisee in us will not always go quietly. He must be forced out by the Holy Spirit's revelatory and sanctifying work.

HYPOCRISY AND THE HOLY SPIRIT

The doctrine of being filled with the Holy Spirit is interpreted in several ways. I don't have time to get into those here and it is not important for this discussion. However, within a popular interpretation of Ephesians 1:13, there is a danger. The passage says, "Having believed, you were marked in him with a seal, the promised Holy Spirit." Those who interpret this passage as saying that all commands to be filled with the Holy Spirit are encapsulated in this promise and therefore, we should not seek any additional fillings because, as some say, "You can't be filled with part of the Holy Spirit! Don't you have all of God you can have when you were saved? How can you have 'part of God' and not all?"

The danger here is that folks are running away from one dangerous extreme to the other. We push them away from a *bear* and right into the paws of a *lion*. The fact is that Christians— even ministers—are struggling with a myriad of sins in our nation in alarming numbers! I won't argue that we are marked and sealed with the Holy Spirit at salvation. But what good does it do to run around saying we are perfectly sanctified and holy based on Ephesians 1:13, and avoid letting the Holy Spirit clean out our hearts as we daily yield to him?

We must daily yield to what is eternally true in order for The Holy Spirit to make immediate changes in the here and now. I recommend Watchman Nee's incredible little book on Paul's letter to the Ephesians, *Sit, Walk, Stand.* As Nee so aptly points out, Ephesians one and two show us that we are seated with Christ in the heavenly realms. Ephesians three and four show us how we are to walk in Christ on a daily basis in light of this revelation of where we are seated. And, Ephesian five and six show us how we are to stand in terms of the daily battle of the Christian life.[4]

We must daily yield to what is eternally true in order for The Holy Spirit to make immediate changes in the here and now.

Many of us are trying to walk and/or stand before having revelation of where we are seated. Others have had revelation of where they are seated, but forget they are commanded therefore to walk and stand. They stop there, thinking they don't have to walk this revelation out in their daily life. Sometimes we hamstring ourselves spiritually because we are caught in a speck of hypocrisy and don't even know it. We have knowledge about what Christ did for us on the cross, but we fail to move on from there to let Christ's work on the cross make us holy, pure, and authentic Christians!

It's as if we don't want to admit there is a problem, because we are afraid to taint the doctrine of our being sealed with the Spirit at salvation. In addition to this, we might as well face the truth of what John says in I John 1:8, "If we claim to be without sin, we deceive ourselves and the truth is not in us. If we confess our sins, he is faithful and just to forgive us our sins and purify us from all unrighteousness. If we claim we have not sinned, we make him out to be a liar and his word has no place in our lives."

In the name of doctrine, we avoid the Spirit of God! That is a recipe for hypocritical disaster!

If we use Ephesians 1:13 to say that we do not need to yield daily to the Holy Spirit's refreshing and purifying power in our lives, we have just experienced a demonic trap. Scripture does not contradict scripture. Scripture interprets scripture. If we hold onto a belief that does not allow us to admit to ourselves (and to God) that we have sinned and need the Spirit's power to be cleansed and renewed, we are sure to put a lid on our souls and avoid our true spiritual condition. The result of this kind of action will always be hypocrisy because we are trying to act as if we are new creations without allowing the Spirit to renew and create us in fresh ways each day. In the name of doctrine, we avoid the Spirit of God! That is a recipe for hypocritical disaster! Perhaps, just perhaps, our interpretation of certain scriptures needs to be refined.

PROPERLY INTERPRETING SCRIPTURE

Whenever I meet people who oppose a properly interpreted scripture with another scripture, I get the feeling they aren't trying to find out what scripture says, but rather they are trying to get scripture to back up what they believe. And, usually when this is the case, the scripture they use is being taken out of context or it has been misinterpreted altogether.

There might be an instance where a doctrinal truth has passed along, and after a time, it takes on a spin, the original truth is warped (be it ever so slightly), and soon we are defending a position that is not based on scripture, but on a traditional interpretation of the scriptures that has a spin on it. The spin is the minute warping of a truth to take someone or something down a dangerous road that leads to error and deception. This is not done intentionally, of course.

The Pharisees did this with the Sabbath day.[5] Perhaps we are doing this with some popularly held beliefs right now. The New Pharisee relies on old traditional views rather than the revealed Word of God on a daily basis to the heart of the believer.

I recently got in a debate with some agnostic kids regarding correct and incorrect interpretations of the Bible. One said, "Well, who is to say which interpretation is right and which one is wrong?" This confusion was holding her back from looking into Christianity further. Even many Christians have a hard time answering that one. But, it is actually easy to answer and vital to one's own faith. I mean, if you cannot interpret scripture accurately and appropriately in your own walk with Christ, you are in trouble! It's not as if you are interpreting hieroglyphics made up by a bunch of religious mystics. The Bible should be read like any other historical piece of literature. We use the laws of interpretation for all literature, not just for the Bible!

You should read and interpret it as it is written. Literature is meant to be taken as the author intends it to be interpreted. Sounds simple, doesn't it?

Sometimes people will be reading the Bible and exclaim to themselves or to others, "God gave me a word when I was reading the Bible today!" Perhaps they read the passage where Jesus decides to go back to Jerusalem (Matthew 20:17, Luke 18: 31–33) and they claim that God has told them to go back to their homes and live with their parents as they read this verse.

...scripture must first and foremost be interpreted as it was meant by the original author.

God may or may not have actually given them that word (sometimes called a *Rhema* word[6]). But first and foremost, that passage is an historical account of Jesus going back to Jerusalem for his triumphal entry. Any secondary interpretations are just that, secondary. Many times, they are misinterpreted personal words that ended up not being a word from God, but the person's own presumptuous wishes. Other times, God can, and does indeed, use scripture to give people personal direction. Regardless, scripture must first and foremost be interpreted as it was meant by the original author.

THE NEW PHARISEE   53

HYPOCRISY IN MINISTRY

Hypocrisy can creep into our lives in other ways besides misinterpreting the Bible. Sometimes we have ulterior motives for certain religious roles or actions. A popular motive for singing or performing in front of a congregation is to be honored and gain acceptance. However, the proper motive for performing in front of a congregation should be to minister in some way to them for the glory of God. Acceptance and honor should be sought from the Lord alone.

Sometimes hypocrisy enters as we develop an idolatrous attachment to a certain person or group. We may form a clique of sorts, and then purposely drive away others who may threaten the closed circle that has been created for the comfort of our clique. How many times have others, maybe even you, walked into a church for the first time and sensed that the people were not that excited that you were there? Perhaps only a few, if any, introduced themselves and maybe you got a cold shoulder and a frown from some. It's not a pleasant experience, is it?

This is the essence of the New Pharisee— hypocrisy.

However hypocrisy enters, it eventually takes shape in our avoidance of the inner life with God. We cover over our wicked hearts and begin creating masks, images, or a fantasy world where we pretend we are a successful, vibrant Christian, even though we may not be. However it takes shape, the bottom line is this: we are clean on the outside, but filthy on the inside. This is the essence of the New Pharisee—hypocrisy.

Most of the time, hypocrisy is a slow shift rather than an immediate condition, just like the frog in the kettle that is boiled so slowly that it never notices until it is too late, it's dead. We avoid the inner life with Christ ever so slowly. One day, we have forgotten what a relationship with God was like. Why do we allow this? How does it happen?

Charles Finney recounts the now famous quote from a renowned actor named David Garrick who was talking with the bishop of London. The bishop asked him why actors could play a fictional part, and yet make everyone cry, while pastors had a hard time getting their people to respond at all. Garrick replied, "It is because we represent fiction as reality, and you represent reality as fiction."[7]

Ouch! That hurts. But was the actor right? Do we wear masks of happiness to cover our pain? Do we let other Christians in our church know when we are going through a difficult time? Do we try to hide the fact that our marriage or family is crumbling?

Perhaps we wear masks to protect ourselves. I do not think putting on an act in church is always a case of being a hypocrite. It could be that a person took a risk, was vulnerable with a few brothers or sisters in Christ, and instead of understanding and keeping this person's private disclosures in confidence, they went around the gossip train with it. If that were to happen to me, I would put on an act in that church as well! Better yet, I would leave that church!

What makes Christians want to spread around somebody else's pain? I think hypocrisy is part of it. The mask of hypocrisy is not being worn by the one being gossiped about in that instance, but by those who gossip. It takes a hypocrite to believe they are better than others are. Since we are all sinners and all of our hearts are wicked above all else (Jeremiah 17:9), those who act as if their hearts are not as deceitful are both arrogant and deceived.

> **We lead the way to Christ and to the kingdom of God when we choose to be honest and reveal our struggles.**

In other instances, we may have an image to keep up, or a mask to wear so that others do not think poorly of us. It could very well be that others will think poorly of us when we live an authentic life, but it is better to be real. For when we are real, we are courageous, genuine, willing to gain the applause of heaven and lose the applause of earth. In a sense, we lead the way to Christ and to the kingdom of God when we choose to be honest and reveal our struggles.

A LESSON FROM JOB

Job is the oldest book in the Bible. It is considered by literary critics throughout the world as one of the most beautifully scripted and poetic of all pieces of classic literature anywhere, ever. Well, it might be a beautiful piece of literature, but it still represents the misery of a guy who most believe got the raw end

---

of the deal. He was one of the few God-fearing people around. He honored God in everything he did. God honored him too. Listen to God's conversation with Satan concerning Job: "Have you considered my servant Job? There is no one on earth like him; he is blameless and upright, a man who fears God and shuns evil." (Job 1:8)

That's a pretty good letter of recommendation from a considerable reference! If *God* says you're a righteous person, you've got it made! So far, so good. This book of Job is a happy book at this point. According to the popular *bless me, God* mindset in certain Christian circles, this book is staying right on target. The first eight verses of this book would indicate that the rest of this classic story is full of instances where the blessings of God poured down on a guy named Job.

If I were Job, I would have thought I was cruising on easy street. I've got my spiritual house in order. God is blessing my socks off materially and physically. Whew! I should take a six-month vacation around the world and celebrate! There's nothing wrong with that. Some of us could use a good vacation.

But the startling thing about Job's life is this: God decided to prune, to prove and test Job. God doesn't tempt us. (James 1:13–15) Satan tempts us. But, God often *tests* us by allowing Satan to *tempt* us. As you know, Job really had a trial of faith. He lost all of his children. He lost all of his possessions. He was reduced to a man full of puss-oozing boils with a wife who was pressed to her wits, and just wanted Job to "curse God and die!" (Job 2:9)

His wife was wrong, of course. But just in case we are tempted to get a little self-righteous about her response, let us remember that she watched all of her babies die and she lost all of her things, and had a husband who was reduced to one big glop of infection. Yuck!

A careful reading of Job will give you several indications of the popular theology of that day. Essentially, the prevailing theology of Job's day was similar to today's popular theology—God blesses you when you are without sin, and he curses you when you are in sin. This theology says that if someone has something bad happen to her, there must be great sin in her life. If something good happens to a person, he must be pleasing God, and God is rewarding him. Have you ever heard that theology before?

Job's friends were very sympathetic and supportive at first. But after a while, they just couldn't take it anymore. They said to one another, "There has to be a reason for this!" Job's three friends were Eliphaz, Bildad, and Zophar. They were probably very righteous men as well to have been so close to Job that they left their homes to go comfort him. They sat with him in mourning for seven days and didn't say a word. (Job 2:11–13) Job cried out in verse three of chapter three, "May the day of my birth perish, and the night it was said, 'A boy is born!' That day—may it turn to darkness; may God above not care about it."

Okay. So, Job was having a bad day. He sunk into a deep depression. Some today say it is a sin to be depressed. I would ask Job, Jeremiah, David, and that one guy we talk about in

Christian circles from time to time—JESUS—about righteous people being depressed before making such a sweeping statement. Read about their lives in scripture, and it is clear that they were deeply troubled individuals on many occasions. I have a hunch that Job's friends (his counselors) believed it was a sin to be depressed. Listen to Eliphaz giving this advice: "Your words have supported those who have stumbled; you have strengthened faltering knees. But now trouble comes to you, and you are discouraged; it strikes you, and you are dismayed. Should not your piety be your confidence and your blameless ways your hope?" (Job 4:4–6)

It's almost as if Eliphaz is saying, "Hey Job! Get over it, would ya? Just hope that it will get better because you are a good guy! Good things happen to good people. Bad things happen to bad people. You're a good person so this shouldn't really be happening. Maybe it's happening because you don't believe that only good things happen to good people and not bad." Eliphaz might as well say, "Job, you are a good person who is allowing bad things to happen to him because you doubt the fact that bad things don't happen to good people!" *Are you confused yet?*

I have a friend who went through a difficult season in his Christian walk (in other words, he experienced the normal Christian life!). He also went through a time of depression. A close friend finally had enough and declared, "Why don't you just get over it?" He had the strongest desire to reply, "Why don't you just get over me not getting over it!" It was as if his friend could take no more, and just had to have him be over his issue. I think the same thing was going on with Job's counselors.

This is the advice that Job got from his best friends while his life was in ruins. I think Job became increasingly impatient because of the incorrect advice of his friends. He tried to do everything he knew, and it didn't seem to change his circumstances one iota. It is clear from the book of Job that Job was a firm believer of the sovereignty of God. Job knew that, ultimately, God was allowing this and could lift this curse any split second that he wanted to lift it.

POP THEOLOGY

It seems like there is always a battle in Christendom between biblical theology and the popular theology of the day. Pop theology can be difficult to deal with, especially when there is a drought of expository teaching and preaching of the Scriptures. The pop theology of Job's day was contradicting his faith in God. In the end, he stood on the fact that God was sovereign and good.

I have found that those who walk the closest with the Lord have a firm belief in the sovereignty and authority of God in their daily life. The truth is you cannot trust God without a belief in his sovereignty, authority, ability, and control of your daily life. Universally, those who have really lived great Christian lives all have this anchor. A preacher once asked Christian author and missionary Elizabeth Elliot what the secret to her success as a Christian has been. She replied, "Trust. What else is there?"[8] Indeed. What else is there?

Job trusted God. His friends, however, seemed to think he didn't dot the right *i* or cross the right *t,* and so now he left himself open to this horrible affliction. Think about that. Can you believe his friends would actually allow themselves to think such a thought, let alone utter it? If I were they, I would be shaking in my shoes! I mean, I am certainly not a perfect Christian; I make mistakes often. If that means God is going to afflict me in the same way as Job, I'm in big trouble! I look at Job's life and walk with God, and I compare my own, and I think Job's got the upper hand on me when it comes to personal righteousness and holiness.

Job's friends could not believe this or say this without secretly thinking that they were better or more righteous than Job. If having no trials equals a life of which God approves, God approves of the lives of Job's friends, but not of Job's life. And, if you believe that, you will think to yourself that you are better than the person who has problems. You will be thinking to yourself, if she were as righteous and together as I was, she wouldn't have all these problems.

There are of course many commentaries on the book of Job. I always think it is humorous to read a particular commentator basically agree with Job's counselors in the commentary. The same pop theology back then is still alive and well today. Some of these misguided commentators are even so brash to suggest that Job was so proud and self-righteous that God really had to give this guy a string of bad luck! Job wasn't self-righteous. Job actually was a man who obeyed very closely the unwritten law of God in his heart and in his actions. Job never looked on women with lustful intentions. Job always did to others what he wanted them to do to him. In fact, at the end God justified Job and rebuked Job's friends. God did not say that he allowed this trial in Job's life because Job was so bad. God allowed it because he knew he could trust Job to honor God. Remember the beginning of the book? Even Satan agreed that Job was a righteous and upright man. Job was not a hypocrite. The entire trial was a test of Job's faith. Christ has told us as Christians that if we are truly his disciples, we will be tried by fire as well. If you are not disciplined, you are not true sons. (Hebrews 12:8)

Today's pop theology, like the theology of Job's friends, says problems and trials happen to those Christians who do not love God as they should. Biblical theology says problems and trials happen to those Christians who love God the most. The Bible says, "We must go through many hardships to enter the king-dom of God." (Acts 14:22)

The New Pharisee hopes to live a life virtually free from problems. The New Pharisee compares his having-it-all-togeth-erness with someone else and concludes that since he has a spouse, two kids, a dog, a cat, and a big house with three-car garage, he must be better and more settled, or trustworthy, or stable. Today's pop theology would say that material, financial, and physical blessings are God's way of saying that he approves of your life. I would argue that spiritual blessings are God's way of saying he loves you as his own child. But he also disciplines those he loves. (Hebrews 12:5–13)

The New Pharisee hopes to live a life virtually free from problems.

I have bad news for the New Pharisee in us who is tempted to think that material, financial, and family blessings are God's stamp of approval on us. *Jesus Christ, Paul, and John the Baptist had none of these things!* According to this analysis, these biblical giants would be considered, unsettled, untrustworthy, and unstable. Sometimes, the next level of discipleship is to have all these things stripped away. And sometimes, the next level after that is to endure scorn and mocking from those who think they are better than we are because they still have all of their possessions and blessings of this world.

There are books currently coming out that seem to emphasize this "bless me" attitude. I am not saying it is wrong to ask God to bless us. I pray for God to bless me all the time. But what do we, as humans, consider blessings? What does God consider blessings? I think we can make a good guess by reading the Bible. Jesus said we were blessed if the following was happening in our lives (Matthew 5:1–12):

1. If you are poor in spirit (broken and humble)
2. If you are mourning
3. If you are meek
4. If you hunger and thirst for righteousness
5. If you are merciful
6. If you are pure in heart
7. If you are a peacemaker

8. If you are persecuted because of righteousness

9. If people insult you, persecute you, and say all kinds of evil
   against you because of Jesus (some people have all manner
   of evil said against them because of themselves)

The beatitudes are what Jesus called the blessings of those
that loved Him. *So when you are asking Jesus to bless you, what
are you really asking?*

I am the first to declare that I do believe that God blesses his
people financially, physically, domestically, and socially. But
surely, he also wants to bless us spiritually. I think we should
reconsider what we are really asking the Lord when we get serious about praying for his blessings. Do we know what we're
asking for?

A Christian friend of mine, who is a new father and married to
a beautiful Christian woman, recently went through a difficult
time with his body. He was in a car accident that left him with a
painful, on-going battle with backaches. His auto insurance
would not cover all of his bills. He is also finding it difficult to do
his job. He said to me, "If you ever ask God to give you patience,
be sure you know what you're asking." I responded, "Why? Have
you been asking God for patience?" He answered, "Yes. I have
asked God to give me patience for several months now. And, here
all this has happened all of a sudden." The good thing is that he
has a confidence in his Lord, and joy on his face as we talked of
the Lord's goodness in spite of difficulties. In a way, I guess we
concluded that he was very blessed.

I'm not saying that God hurt my friend, or that God caused
the accident. But, I *am* saying that God is sovereign over the

lives of those who want him to be, and will answer prayers
because he is a prayer answering God! Proverbs 20:24 says, "A
man's steps are directed by the Lord. How then can anyone
understand his own way?"

MODERN-DAY JOB

An all-too-common experience in the church today is a replay
of this same interaction of feelings, thoughts, and attitudes
between Christians who have, and Christians who have not.
Imagine the following scenario:

> A Christian woman finds out her husband is leaving her and
> the family to go run off with his secretary. She suddenly needs a
> second job, and has to move into a lower-income area to afford
> the rent. The kids don't dress as nicely as they used to, and they
> seem more quiet and sad now. The woman finally breaks under
> the pressure, and comes to church a wreck. She confides in
> some Christian friends at her church. They try to be of help to
> her. But after several months of her depression and struggles,
> they begin to judge her, and think themselves a little better than
> she because they always have the joy of the Lord as they drive to
> and from church with their financially successful husbands, and
> happy, obedient kids. The overwhelmed woman feels less spiri-
> tual, so she goes to counseling to find out what is wrong with
> her. The counselor has her reading books and listening to CDs,
> but she still is so tired and sad all the time. Other than working
> sixty hours a week, driving the kids to school and work, clean-
> ing the house, mowing the lawn, fixing broken cars, and writing
> requests for extensions to bill collectors, she really has no rea-
> son to be tired. The married ladies still invite her to their Bible
> studies, but they are concerned that she is not at their level of
> spirituality. They notice that she cries often and always worries

about finding a mate, even though it's only been seven years since her husband divorced her. They decide it is best to just have their Bible study for the more mature women, and maybe tell her they will pray for her.

Wouldn't it be interesting to go back seven years and replay this scene in heaven? Some angel says to the Lord, "Lord, who is ready to go to the next level of discipleship and intimacy with you?" The Lord replies, "You see this woman here? Her heart is a heart of gold. There is no ill will inside of her, and she is a true daughter of mine with excellent character." The angel returns, "Lord, Satan is asking whom he might sift. What shall our response be?" God says, "Tell him he can sift my precious daughter here. I cannot find another who is as ready as she is. I am going to make her even more wonderful and wise than she is already. In due time, I will build her back up. For now, I will let her be broken." "Yes, Father."

Isn't that what happened with Job?

In the end, God restored to Job many times over what he had before. Job was finally blessed in the end. *But what about the trial?* Did he receive any blessings *during* the trial? According to Jesus' teaching on the beatitudes, Job was very blessed during that trial. And what did he learn about trials through all this? He learned that God could do whatever he wants. He learned that we do not always have to know the reasons for the things God allows in our lives. He learned that when bad things are happening, it does not necessarily mean a person has done anything wrong. In some cases, it can mean a person is doing something right.

Wait a minute! That is quite disconcerting! You mean to say that I could be going about trying to please God and obey him, and a tragedy could still strike my life? I mean to say that tragedy strikes everyone. The rain falls on the just and unjust. One of my all-time favorite characters, the dreaded Pirate Roberts, from one of my all-time favorite movies, *The Princess Bride,* says, "Life is pain, your highness. Anybody who says anything else is just selling something."[9]

I like that. If you ever hear a Christian or even yourself saying anything else, ask yourself what it is you are selling. You certainly aren't selling Christ. Tell the New Pharisee inside that she will no longer rule in you with pride and self-reliance. Tell the New Pharisee within yourself that you will no longer simply live according to pop theology. The New Pharisee will be dethroned and Christ will take residence instead!

PLUCK OUT THE PLANK—SEE THE SPECK

Have you ever experienced someone judging you or your heart? I hope you never have to go through that. Unfortunately, we live in a world where that is a constant scenario. Man has a tendency towards judging his fellow man.

> **Tell the New Pharisee within yourself that you will no longer simply live according to pop theology.**

Jesus addressed this many times in the Gospels. He said this regarding judging others in his sermon on the mount in Matthew 7:3–6:

Why do you look at the speck of sawdust in your brother's eye and pay no attention to the plank in your own eye? How can you say to your brother, "Let me take the speck out of your eye," when all the time there is a plank in your own eye? You hypocrite, first take the plank out of your own eye, and then you will see clearly to remove the speck from your brother's eye.

I believe the plank is the sin of judging. Jesus condemned the Pharisees for this sin. In fact, all the denunciations he handed to the Pharisees regarding how they treated their fellow man and woman can be traced back to this root sin—pride. *Pride is the seed for the sin of judging.*

This is not to be confused with judging fruit. In that case, we are commanded to judge fruit and, in a discipleship sense especially, we must be willing to confront one another in love with the truth. This is what Jesus is doing with the Pharisees. Surely, he is not accusing the Pharisees of being hypocrites because they judge, if what he is saying to them is judgmental itself! Talk about hypocrisy!

The sin of judging is not telling others the truth. The sin of judging is the prideful self-exalting attitudes and actions within us, and the out-workings of that sinful judgment that we convey to others. When we think that we are better than others are because of certain sins or weaknesses they have, we can be sure that we have the greater sin. When we judge another as being not quite as righteous as we are because of a particular misdeed or character flaw, we can be sure that we have the greater unrighteousness.

Another way of saying this is that out of all sins, pride and self-righteousness are the worst. The reason the Pharisees were condemned was not because they were committing sinful acts.

They weren't. Rather, they were condemned because, though they did not commit certain fleshly sins, they thought they were better than others who did. *This is the plank.* Anytime a person confronts another about a sin or misdeed with an attitude of pride or self-righteousness, he or she has a weightier sin than the sin they confront in the sinful person.

Let's do an exercise to demonstrate this: I have done this exercise a number of times in my years as a youth minister and evangelist. Go find a two-by-four, at least four feet in length. Then grab a friend or willing participant and have him sit in a chair opposite you while you are sitting in your chair. Now, grab the two-by-four and put it in front of your face. You should slightly resemble a hammerhead shark. Okay. Go ahead and get any residual laughs out at this point. If you are doing this on stage at a church or youth room, ham it up a bit, and script a conversation that has to do with one friend confronting another about a particular sin. Now reach out to the person you are confronting as you hold the two-by-four in front of your eyes. Say something like, "Look friend, I have been noticing that piece of sawdust in your eyes, and it's really bothering me. It looks bad and frankly, I'm embarrassed to be seen in public with you. You've got a piece of sawdust dangling from your eye! You ought to be ashamed of yourself!"

The room will find this very humorous. If they are silent, perhaps the humorous lesson hit too close to home. But that's okay, too.

It may be humorous to watch a person with a board in his face trying to tell someone else he has a sliver in his, but that is what we are doing when we judge someone else. Notice that Jesus also calls this hypocrisy. Again, it has to do with playing a part as an actor—we are pretending to be someone we're not!

CLEANING THE OUTSIDE OF THE CUP

Jesus used many powerful images as he described the Pharisees' problem with hypocrisy in Matthew 23. One of the most powerful is the symbolism of the cup being clean. Obviously, we are the cup. The outside of the cup is the outward presentation, what others see. The inside of the cup is our hearts, what God sees. Jesus was angry at the Pharisees for only worrying about what others see and not about what God sees.

I once played a mad scientist in a sketch. It was a humorous sketch about a mad scientist who was trying to create a potion that, if ingested, would give the person a desire to do the things of God. I probably overacted the part. I must admit, it was very enjoyable to jump into this character and see things from his point of view. The biggest surprise to my performance was the reaction of my friends. They were shocked to see me play someone who was so different from me. In fact, I believe I detected a slight hesitation in some of them to talk to me for several days after that. It wasn't that I offended them. They couldn't stop talking about the sketch for days. But, you see, I confused them because I became a totally different person on stage. They had never known that part of me.

Acting a part that is different from what is true of you can throw people off. They might see you as two-faced, a bit fake, or plastic. The classic public examples we have of this, unfortunately, are of the American TV evangelists of the late 1980s who accused each other of sin. Within months, many of them were caught in the very sins of which they were accusing others. Their supporters were let down and angry that they had been fooled. The outside presentation was not true of the inside situation. These evangelists had merely cleaned the outside of the cup.

The New Pharisee avoids the uncleanliness of the heart by emphasizing a certain list of outward prohibitions.

Cleaning the outside of the cup has more applications than just acting. We emphasize cleaning the outside of the cup when we address certain vices such as smoking, drinking alcohol, watching movies, dancing, tattoos, shaved heads, listening to certain types of music, and even certain styles of dress. To be sure, some of these practices can be very dangerous and very destructive. But the Bible has no prohibition on any of these actions other than drunkenness. Too much smoking can give you lung cancer. Too much drinking can lead to drunkenness and a host of dangers in that state of being. Wearing revealing clothing can attract the wrong kind of attention from others and can tempt others to lust. Dancing can be negative when it becomes suggestive and lustful as well. But clearly, there were dancing, drinking and wearing of attractive clothing by the people of God in the Bible. I am sure a new bride wore an attractive dress at her wedding.

The New Pharisee decides not to do these things for cleaning the outside of the cup. An authentic Christian really isn't very concerned with cleaning the outside of the cup. The New Pharisee avoids the uncleanliness of the heart by emphasizing a certain list of outward prohibitions. The authentic Christian desires God to clean his inner wickedness, impurity, thoughts, desires, and motives. The New Pharisee finds pleasure in others seeing her as especially clean by the way she acts, dresses, talks, and denies herself of certain pleasures. The authentic Christian realizes that by letting the Lord clean him on the inside, he will know what God wants him to do or not do on the outside.

To find out who you are most like, ask yourself, "who makes me angry?"

New Pharisees are able to look better on the outside because that is their only focus. Authentic Christians are so full of joy at what the Lord has done for them on the inside that they know which things on the outside are important to the Lord, and what is free for them to enjoy. New Pharisees proudly display the list of prohibitions for others to take note and do likewise. Authentic Christians sometimes will appear to be sinful by not following these same prohibitions. New Pharisees judge the authentic Christians. Authentic Christians pray for New Pharisees.

Here is an interesting litmus test: the Pharisees were angry with the sinners. Jesus was angry with the Pharisees. To find out who you are most like, ask yourself, "who makes me angry?"

The New Pharisee within us will always exist if, and when, we allow hypocrisy into our lives. When we come before the Lord in humility, sincerity, and openness, we will find he is pleased to take residence and abide in our hearts. This is the greatest miracle there is! Now when the Lord takes up residence inside us, he will begin a series of remodeling projects. This is not something you have to do. He may ask you to help him. He certainly will ask you to obey him every time he shows you the truth. Holiness is the result of simply loving and obeying the Father. The inside of the cup is cleaned as we allow the Lord to reign in us! Lord, reign in our mortal bodies by faith!

Pastor Otis Lockett says, "You can't get victory by tryin' to get victory!"[10] I agree. We are not able to clean the inside of our cup. We don't have the power. "Then why are you telling me this? If I can't do it, why tell me about it?" Listen to this promise in God's Word: "The same power that raised Jesus Christ from the dead will also give life to your mortal bodies!" (Romans 8:11) Isn't that wonderful? We have access to the power that raised Christ from the dead!

Joyce Meyer testifies to this principle in *Knowing God Intimately: Being as Close to Him as You Want to Be:* "I have to confess that, in ignorance, there were many years when I diligently sought God for His power. I wanted to see signs, wonders, and miracles and have authority over evil spirits and do great and mighty things in Jesus' name; but I was an 'outer' Christian. I was a spirit-baptized Christian for at least ten years before I understood much at all about the inner life. Then God began to teach me that His kingdom was within me. As I allowed Jesus to rule over my inner life, I began to see more power in my outer life."[11]

I had the opportunity to travel to India several years ago. We were going with a team from a missions organization that specializes in working with the poorest of the poor. Along our journey through that beautiful country, we stopped at a leper home. Actually, it was a large housing unit for hundreds of lepers. It was obviously sad to see these dear people afflicted and made outcasts by society. We quickly discovered from the leaders of this center that we could touch the lepers without fear of getting the disease. Leprosy is curable with medicine that is accessible in North America. Leprosy is caused by a bacterium inside the body. In other words, the way to treat it is not to try to clean up the outside, but to kill the bacterium on the inside. You kill the bacterium on the inside, and the outside will be clean.

In the same way, God wants us to deal with the root cause of sin, and not just cover it over. Just like the lepers of old, we can put wrappings on an infected sore, or we can cure the root cause. The root cause of sin in our lives is not on the outside. The root cause is within us. Our carnal nature is completely corrupted. Christ dealt with this root cause on the cross. He declared, "It is finished!" (John 19:30) And it is! We don't have to focus on the outside of the cup. If we allow Christ to appropriate the work he completed on the cross from within us, we can clean the inside of the cup. Then, the outside will be clean! Alleluia! Amen!

4

Avoiding Sinners

I was in ninth grade. I was shy. I was not a popular kid for a lot of reasons. First, I was almost a year younger than other kids were in my class. Second, I was overweight at the time. I always sat at the back of the room. German class was no different. I sat next to a girl in the back row. We will call her Carrie for now even though that wasn't her real name. I really liked Carrie. We would talk and laugh. She was one of the few popular people who were willing to associate with me. Well, you probably know how ninth grade crushes can be. I also had this gargantuan infatuation with one of the girls in our German class whom we will call Rebecca. Rebecca was pretty, but there was more to my infatuation with Rebecca than just looks. I would develop these infatuations with girls who were cute, but not necessarily beautiful. Anyway, one day as Carrie and I were talking in the back row, Rebecca walked in. My heart went pitter-patter as it usually did when Rebecca was in sight. She looked at Carrie sitting next to me and said, "Hey Carrie! Come sit up here! Don't sit back there with all the losers!" Now, I am not sure of the exact rate in which my infatuation with Rebecca subsided, but let's just say it took around two point seven seconds.

So much for Rebecca. So much for Carrie. She went and sat up front with Rebecca for the rest of the semester. I was humiliated. The classroom stretched out to a quarter-mile long right before my eyes. At least, that's how it felt to me. We can be so cruel to people without even knowing it. Why are we so clueless when it comes to sensitivity and compassion for others?

In Matthew 9:9–13, we find Jesus hanging out with some people who were generally ignored and avoided by the religious community:

> As Jesus went on from there, he saw a man named Matthew sitting at the tax collector's booth. "Follow me," he told him, and Matthew got up and followed him. While Jesus was having dinner at Matthew's house, many tax collectors and sinners came and ate with him and his disciples. When the Pharisees saw this, they asked his disciples, "Why does your teacher eat with tax collectors and sinners?" On hearing this, Jesus said, "It is not the healthy who need a doctor, but the sick. But go and learn what this means: 'I desire mercy, not sacrifice.' For I have not come to call the righteous, but sinners."

What is humorous about this is that one of the sinners that the Pharisees were referring to just happens to be the human author of this book, the Gospel according to Matthew! I am sure Matthew felt the same way I felt when Rebecca effectively called me a loser. I felt rejected by Rebecca and the popular crowd as well. I think the sinners felt rejected by the entire religious community. No doubt, they had heard these kinds of condescending remarks many times before.

AVOID SIN—AVOID SINNERS

The Pharisees kept their distance from people they considered sinners. Because the focus of a hypocrite is all about externals and appearances, the Pharisees did not want to be seen with sinners. They did not appear to be as spiritual when seen near those who did not look clean and holy externally. An entire spiritual paradigm was created by the hypocrisy of the Pharisees. Everything had to have an outward appearance of holiness or spirituality, or the Pharisees kept their distance. When Jesus began spending large amounts of time with the sinners, the Pharisees were sure that they were more righteous than Jesus was. Therefore, their own self-righteous views would not allow them to consider Christ as Messiah. Surely, they would find the Messiah more holy than they were.

An entire spiritual paradigm was created by the hypocrisy of the Pharisees.

Let's take a closer look at these sinners such as Matthew the tax collector. Who are they really? When you strip away all of the outward trappings, we are all the same. Before the Lord, we are all sinful men. Even Isaiah, when he saw the Lord, declared, "Woe to me! I am ruined! For I am a man of unclean lips, and I live among a people of unclean lips, and my eyes have seen the

King, the Lord Almighty." (Isaiah 6:5) The New Pharisee is
deceived into thinking that he is more righteous than people
popularly seen as sinners are. But the truth is, before the Lord,
we are all sinful men and women.

In the Lord's presence, we become aware of our absolute spiritual bankruptcy. We have nothing good in us apart from Christ.
The prophets of the Old Testament all had this same broken attitude about their own sin and the sins of others. They did not
prophesy with a condescending approach. They spoke to the
people as one of them. The Pharisees apparently had either forgotten this fact or missed it altogether.

Had they forgotten about the Rahab the harlot who threw
down the scarlet cord in the town of Jericho? (Joshua 2:21) Her
act of faith allowed Israel to march around Jericho and overtake
it as God brought the walls down. She is even recorded in the
hall of faith in Hebrews 11:31. Even Elijah, one of the greatest
figures in Judaism, spent time in the house of the Gentile widow
of Zarephath. (I Kings 17:7) The prophets of the Old Testament
did not consider themselves too holy to be in the presence of
sinners. The Pharisees did.

New Pharisees have a similar attitude about people in general. They avoid contact with people who drink, smoke, or do
immoral things. The basic message is this: "Don't come around
us until you've cleaned yourself up." And the New Pharisee has
rules, too. Imagine walking into a church on a Sunday morning
and seeing ushers stand and read the following list: "Attention
ladies and gentlemen! Welcome to Friendship Church! Please
observe the following rules: Dress nicely in church, no tattoos,

no body piercings, no hats, no vices, and no weaknesses! You are welcome here if you are able to avoid all of these things. You will notice the exits to your right and left. There are also two exits in the back. In the event of a sinful thought or habit in your life, please make your way through the exits as quickly and inconspicuously as possible. When you have finally arrived spiritually, we welcome you back to Friendship Church. Now we invite you to sit back and enjoy the show!"

We sometimes catch ourselves in a tension between spending too much time in company that can corrupt us, and reaching out to people who are hopelessly lost without contact from us. This is a tension; there is no question about it. But is it right to avoid sinners completely? I don't think we can say that it is in light of the scriptures.

In Harper Lee's world-renowned book, *To Kill a Mockingbird,* Boo Radley was known as a fearful villain, a veritable monster terrorizing the entire neighborhood. Children had terrible nightmares of Boo Radley attacking them in the night. Adults prohibited their children from playing near the Radley house. Intertwined in the Boo Radley scenario was a scandalous court case taking place in town. A black man was going to trial for being falsely accused of raping a white girl. His defense attorney, Atticus Finch, decided to defend him even though he knew it would mean persecution by many in the entire county. On one occasion, Atticus was discussing with his children a bit of advice his father gave him about being kind to others who may seem a bit different than the rest of us. Atticus said that his father allowed his children to shoot certain animals, but claimed it was

a sin to kill a mockingbird because all they do all day long is try
to brighten up the day and "sing their hearts out for us."

Atticus' family found out the hard way that the townspeople
had not learned that same lesson. The people whom the town
feared the most ended up being kind and harmless individuals.
In fact, in spite of their persecution, these feared personalities
still attempted to do good to their fellow man. Boo saved the life
of Atticus Finch's daughter, Scout, even though protecting Scout
meant killing her assailant in self-defense. Scout was happy to
see that Boo was not going to be charged with a crime. She said
to her father, "It would kind of be like killing a mockingbird,
wouldn't it?"[1]

Harper Lee's tale has been mandatory reading for almost
every teenager who attends public school in America, and it has
been published in many languages throughout the world. That
book and the movie forever changed my thinking about people
different from me. It gave me understanding and compassion
for people very different from myself, and it took away the
demonization of sinners and bad people in my mind.

DANIEL AND NEBUCHADNEZZAR

It is clear from the Bible that God loves even the worst kinds
of people. One of the fiercest and most heinous persons in all of
scripture has to be King Nebuchadnezzar of Babylon. This man
was an ambitious, irreverent, and pompous murderer of thousands. Every time his armies invaded another country, there was
mass disaster. In fact, there is very little difference between him

and Herod, who served John the Baptist's head on a platter. At least, that is how it appears.

But there must have been something different about Nebuchadnezzar. Jeremiah prophesies about him, "For I am bringing disaster from the north, even terrible destruction. A lion has come out of his liar; a destroyer of nations has set out." (Jeremiah 4:6–7) Why did Jeremiah continue to prophesy that God called Nebuchadnezzar "My servant Nebuchadnezzar king of Babylon?" (Jeremiah 25:9) Isn't that strange? He calls a wicked Gentile king "My servant." Nebuchadnezzar was in no way a righteous man at this point. Did God see something in Nebuchadnezzar that no man had ever seen? Probably. But God also knew how he was going to humiliate and break Nebuchadnezzar after he captured and destroyed Judah.

Look at the changes in King Nebuchadnezzar before and after meeting the Hebrew men of God:

Before: Nebuchadnezzar built the image of gold of himself that was ninety feet tall. He commanded Daniel's friends, Shadrach, Meshach, and Abednego, to worship or be thrown into the fiery furnace. Nebuchadnezzar said, "Is it true, Shadrach, Meshach, and Abednego that you do not serve my gods or worship the image of gold I have set up?" (Daniel 3:14) Nebuchadnezzar was an arrogant, idolatrous tyrant who became so furious with these three Hebrews that he threw them into the furnace. You know the story. The prideful king was humbled when he saw that they were not touched at all in the furnace, even though the flames from the furnace were killing people outside of the furnace! So what does this passage tell us in terms of convincing unbelievers of God's glory? Maybe we need to be thrown into a few furnaces so that today's unbeliever will be convinced of the Gospel of Christ. It's just a thought.

After: Nebuchadnezzar was warned in a dream that God was about to really humble him. Daniel interpreted his dream: "You will be driven away from people and will live with the wild animals; you will eat grass like cattle and be drenched with the dew of heaven. Seven times will pass by for you until you acknowledge that the Most High is sovereign over the kingdoms of men and gives them to anyone he wishes...Therefore, O king, be pleased to accept my advice: Renounce your sins by doing what is right, and your wickedness by being kind to the oppressed. It may be that then your prosperity will continue." (Daniel 19:25–27) That is exactly what happened to Nebuchadnezzar. He became an animal and was completely humbled. We read of his acknowledgement of God's worth and honor in Daniel 4:34–35. His declaration of praise seems like something Moses or Elijah would say. Isn't this amazing?

We will most likely see Nebuchadnezzar among the saints of God in heaven for eternity. And I can't think of a human being who was more terrible than he was.

> **We will most likely see Nebuchadnezzar among the saints of God in heaven for eternity.**

LOVE THY NEIGHBOR

I'm sure you have read of other wicked people who became godly people in the Bible. Mary Magdalene was a prostitute who became a disciple. She was the first to see Jesus after his resurrection, and had the faith to convince the disciples that Jesus had been raised from the dead (John 20:1). The Samaritan woman at the well was a Gentile and an immoral woman. Jesus broke several social taboos to sit with her and tell her how to be saved. She not only accepted the message, but also spread it throughout her whole town. (John 4:39–42) Think of this! This sinful woman was used of God to evangelize an entire community!

We don't have time to look at the widow of Zeraphath, Rahab the harlot, Darius the Mede, and many other Gentiles who were God's servants in the Old Testament! This was before God had declared to Peter that Gentiles were no longer unclean! In other words, even before God formally declared to his people that Gentiles were clean, he was choosing to reveal himself to specific Gentiles that seemed to have a hunger to know him! He was breaking his own rules when the higher law of love dictated that it be so—even in the old covenant paradigm!

And in the New Testament, God chose Saul of Tarsus, that Pharisee and Hebrew of Hebrews, to bring the Gospel to the Gentiles. God apparently was so eager to show his love to Caesar that he sent Paul through a barrage of storms just to get him before this Gentile ruler. (Acts 23:11; 27:24)

SUPPORT YOUR LOCAL GENTILE

So what does all of this mean to you and me? I think it is quite clear from the Bible that God loves all people. God loves sinners! This message is all through the Old and New Testaments. And frequently, God was breaking his own rules to show sinners his love. So who are the Gentiles anyway?

The word Gentile actually comes from the Greek word *ethne,* where we get nations. So technically, Gentiles are simply the people of all nations of the earth. In Genesis 12:3, we see God promising Abram that "all peoples (*ta ethne,* all ethnic groups) on earth will be blessed through you." Abram is the father of the Gentiles in the sense that he is the father of all nations.

Gentile was a good word from the beginning. Eventually, Gentiles got a bad rap for their intermarriage with Jews. God forbade Israel to intermarry with Gentiles because the Gentiles indeed were idolatrous people with corrupted minds and hearts. Israel compromised to the extent that "the people engaged in all the detestable practices of the nations the Lord had driven out before the Israelites." (I Kings 14:24)

This tendency toward compromise on the part of the Israelites warranted strict commands to stay away from the Gentiles, even though God had shown his ultimate purpose to Abram that he wanted all nations to be blessed. That *was and is* his heart.

Unfortunately, the people of Israel had not learned the proper social boundaries with the Gentiles. The book of Ezra (as well as Nehemiah) tells the story of the Jewish return from exile in Babylon (under Nebuchadnezzar and his successors) and of their purification. They dedicated the rebuilt temple in 516 BC. Ezra taught the people the law and led them in confession and repentance. Ezra 6:21 records that "The Israelites who had returned from the exile ate it (the Passover lamb), together with all who had separated themselves from the unclean practices of their Gentile neighbors in order to seek the Lord, the God of Israel."

Over a period of time, this separation from Gentiles created a self-righteous attitude on the part of the Pharisees. What started out as an attempt to rid themselves of unclean practices eventually created hypocrisy. By the time Christ came on the scene, the Gentiles were regarded as sinful people who were unclean. One was not to be seen in close proximity with them. To call someone a Gentile became an insult. The Gentiles were objects of scorn.

God never meant for it to be taken that way. It is one thing to have intimate relationships with people who live immoral lives. It is another to avoid them completely.

How can we keep away from those for whom Christ died...?

I once counseled a Christian young woman who was dating a man who was not a Christian. She really loved him, but saw compromises taking place in her life because of her relationship with him. I warned her about going too much further with him because it was eating away at her relationship with the Lord. In addition to this, the Bible says not to be unequally yoked with unbelievers. (2 Corinthians 6:14) I was not saying that she was better than he was, or that I was better than he was. But I *was* saying that an intimate relationship with someone who is a bad influence is not good for us—or what God wants.

In fact, there are situations in which God would not want either party in relationship so that he could bring each individual closer to him without distractions. But again, this is not to say that Christians should keep away from unbelievers. How can we keep away from those for whom Christ died, and whom He commands us to go out and love? (Matthew 28:18-20)

New Pharisees eliminate relationships with today's Gentiles, sinners—completely. New Pharisees stay in the comfort of their surroundings like the Pharisees of old and only reach out to those who are of similar outward status and appearance. New Pharisees are like the Israelites who became so afraid of being contaminated that they have removed themselves from any connection to those who may contaminate them.

This is bad news for Gentiles ("How shall they hear without a preacher?" Romans 10:14), for they can find life only in Christ. But it is also bad news for New Pharisees because we will be judged for failing to bring the Gospel to the unsaved! We must rediscover the proper boundaries for relationship with sinners.

BOUNDARIES WITH "GENTILES"

When I was first saved, all my friends were wild party animals. I have to admit, I had a blast with them. To this day, I consider many of them to be the best friends I have ever had. But it was hard for me to know how to relate to them with my newfound faith. Should I have nothing to do with them? Should I still go to bars with them? Should I still party with them?

You know what? I love these questions. I love that we, as Christians, don't have any easy answers to these questions. I love that we have to struggle with these questions to find the right boundaries! Jesus obviously dealt with these same questions. He seemed to have found a way to be with the sinners so much that he was considered one of them. (Luke 19:7; Matthew 9:11) In fact, Jesus referred to this accusation in Matthew 11:19: "The Son of Man came eating and drinking, and they say, 'Here is a glutton and a drunkard, a friend of tax collectors and sinners.'" He was accused of being a sinner because he made friendships with sinners. He did not choose to keep away from sinners.

This is what I mean by *boundaries*. The Israelites ceased relationships with Gentiles during the rebuilding of the temple. But, this was because they were unequally yoked with Gentiles. The Pharisees continued this tradition. They *should have* been forming relationships with Gentiles all along. They were offended with Jesus Christ when he rediscovered the proper balance between relationship and conformity to people's immoral lifestyles.

It is clear that the Pharisees kept themselves at a distance from the Gentiles. In fact, they had no love for these people at all. New Pharisees have a lack of compassion for the lost sinners of this world. New Pharisees within us have a very hard time with those of especially sinful repute. In Jesus' day, it was the tax collector, prostitute and the leper. Today, it seems to be the homosexual or lesbian, the drug dealer, gang member, dope addict or the alcoholic. These are the sinners we really avoid.

It is tough to be a sinner in today's Christian community. We have picket sign demonstrations that declare our stance on abortion. I am sure anyone who is pro-abortion or who has had an abortion at any time in his or her life would shy away from us simply to avoid condemnation. We have also let homosexuals know where we stand in the documents we sign and the statements we make. It would be difficult for anyone struggling with these issues to let anyone in the church know that they are struggling.

We let poor, unsightly beggars know we really don't have time for them. We don't want to be taken advantage of, and we certainly don't want to contribute to any kind of laziness on their part. We have let the world know where we stand. We won't compromise. Okay. So, what does that mean? Did Jesus let the sinners of his day know where he stood? Did he have to? Scripture indicates that Jesus more often made relationships with sinners, and seldom let them know where he stood.

A man I will call Brian walked into the church I used to attend one Sunday morning. He enjoyed the services. He eventually began to bring his whole family. There was one problem: he smoked. In fact, I guess he did not know that people were not supposed to smoke if they were churchgoers. Nobody told him. He would come to service projects with the church and smoke as he painted the church building. But still, nobody told him he couldn't smoke and be part of the body of Christ. He had become a Christian soon after he began attending. After about a year, he just stopped smoking. And after a couple years, he began teaching Sunday school and preaching in the pastor's absence. He took Bible and theology courses for several years, and eventually became the Associate Pastor of this same church. I remember Brian speaking to the church one day. He thanked everyone for not judging him, but showing him Christ's love instead. He told them that he probably would have left the church if someone had made a comment regarding his smoking.

When I think of Brian, I think of an example where relationships made it unnecessary to have to let Brian know where we stood on the issue of smoking, rock music, abortion, alcoholism, and a host of other things. Jesus only seemed to want the Pharisees to know where He stood. The Pharisees wanted the sinners to know where they stood. The New Pharisee is most concerned that the sinners change their habits and appearance. The New Pharisee is not concerned with forming a relationship with sinners.

In Luke 18:9–14, Jesus told the parable of a proud Pharisee and a remorseful tax collector. Of course, tax collectors in Jesus' day were almost considered scum because they worked for the evil Roman Empire and extracted heavy taxes from their own countrymen. The Jews felt that tax collectors were traitors. The reputation of tax collectors was similar to today's lawyer.

The New Pharisee is not concerned with forming a relationship with sinners.

Jesus chose these two kinds of people for this parable because he wanted to confront those "who were confident of their own righteousness." (Luke 18:9) Philip Yancey, in his monumental book *The Jesus I Never Knew,* notes that this parable "Captures the inclusive gospel of grace in a nutshell. The Pharisee, who fasted twice a week and tithed on schedule, piously thanked God that he was above robbers, evildoers, and

adulterers and far above the tax collector standing to the side.
The tax collector, too humiliated even to raise his eyes to
heaven, prayed the simplest prayer possible, 'God, have mercy
on me, a sinner.' Jesus drew the conclusion, 'I tell you that this
man, rather than the other, went home justified before God.'"
Yancey goes on to say that although "Behavior matters in many
ways; it simply is not how to get accepted by God."[2]

THE GOOD SAMARITAN

When Jesus felt that people didn't have a clue, he told a parable. It's almost as if he said, "I don't know how else to explain
this to you people! Don't you get it? Ummm. Okay. Let me tell
you a story." Jesus was perhaps the greatest storyteller. To be
sure, he told the greatest stories! Parables have a way of getting
inside the heart and soul. They bring us along with our full
attention. They create images in our mind, and we are carried
along in our imaginations by the storytellers. We must go wherever he wants to take us because the story has that kind of
power. We may not like where we end up. But, we have to come
along nevertheless.

A young lawyer was eager to prove to Jesus that he was completely obedient to the ten commandments. Jesus tested him by
saying, "Do this (love the Lord your God with all your heart and
all your soul and with all your strength and with all your mind,
and love your neighbor as yourself) and you will live." The lawyer asked, "And who is my neighbor?" Jesus told the parable of
the Samaritan in order to show this man that, although he
thought he had been completely obedient to the law of Moses, he

had not loved his neighbor; therefore, he had not loved the Lord with all his heart, soul, mind and strength. (Luke 10:30–37)

It is scary to think that our hearts can be so cold, and yet we can be so clueless of our true state before God. It's not that this young lawyer was trying to trick anyone—he sincerely thought he was obedient to all that God had commanded. He would never have believed that he was so far from God. Jesus told this parable to reveal to this young man just how far he was from loving God or his neighbor.

Sincerity isn't enough. We must be more than sincere. We must know the truth and have our true state be revealed to us. Otherwise, we will be like this young lawyer—*sincere and blind* at the same time. He probably avoided the sinners like everyone else. It was most likely the first time he ever heard that loving his neighbor included loving people of another race, culture, creed, and socio-economic status; this love had to be to the point that he actually met their physical needs. Jesus tried to show the Jews why it was so wrong to avoid the sinners, but they didn't get it. He tried to show them that people commonly considered sinners were capable of as much good as they were, but they were clueless. So, he told the parable of the good Samaritan.

You have to understand that Samaritans were looked down upon for the following reasons:

1. They were Gentiles.
2. They were considered a lower race of people by the Jews.
3. They had their own temple and place of worship (probably on Mount Gerizim, John 4:20; Deuteronomy 11:29).

In Luke 10:30–37, the parable of the good Samaritan is
recorded. An expert in the law was questioning Jesus. He
wanted to know the right answers to Jesus' questions. Jesus then
tells the story of a man who was beaten as he walked along the
road from Jerusalem to Jericho. A priest and a Levite walked
past the man but did not help him. In verse 33, Jesus says, "But
a Samaritan, as he traveled, came where the man was; and when
he saw him, he took pity on him." The Samaritan bound up his
wounds and took care of him. Jesus asks in verse 36, "Which of
these three do you think was a neighbor to the man who fell into
the hands of robbers?" In verse 37, we read the response of the
expert in the law: "The one who had mercy on him." Jesus told
him, "Go, and do likewise." Wouldn't Jesus say the same thing
to you and me today? Go and do likewise.

Charles Colson recounts the confession of the pastor of a
large mega-church in *The Body:*

> The late Max Cadenhead, when he was pastor of First Baptist
> Church in Naples, Florida, riveted his congregation one day
> with a bold confession. "My message today is on the parable of
> the Good Samaritan," Max announced. "Let me start with an
> illustration. Remember last year when the Browns came forward
> to join the church?" he asked. Everyone nodded; the Browns
> were a very influential family. "Well the same day a young man
> came forward and gave his life to Christ. I could tell he needed
> help—and we counseled him." No heads nodded; no one
> remembered. "We worked with the Browns, got them onto com-
> mittees. They've been wonderful folks," Cadenhead said to muf-
> fled amen's. "And the young man…well, we lost track. Until
> yesterday, that is, as I was preparing today's message on the
> good Samaritan. I picked up the paper, and there was that young

man's picture. He had shot and killed an elderly woman." Chins dropped throughout the congregation, mine (Colson's) included, as the pastor continued. "I never followed up on that young man, so I am the priest who saw the man in trouble and crossed to the other side of the road. I am a hypocrite." More of that kind of sober honesty in the church would be very healthy. For God's kingdom is just the opposite of ours. We go after the rich or the influential, thinking if we can just bag this one or that one, we'll have a real catch for the kingdom. Like the folks profiled by the apostle James (James 2:1-13), we offer our head tables to the wealthy and well-dressed and reserve the back seats for those we consider unimportant.[3]

New Pharisees want to rub shoulders with the important people. New Pharisees want to know the proper biblical answers so that we can teach them to others in Sunday school classes, Bible studies, or preach behind the pulpit. We're not completely sure why the expert in the law wanted to know that right answer. Jesus wanted him to know the answer so that he could "Go and do likewise."

I think that is what Jesus would say to us. The New Pharisee inside of us wants to avoid sinners and to judge them from afar. Jesus wants to move us out of our comfort zones. He would have us learn what it is to find boundaries in relationships with even those entangled in the grossest of sins. He would have us realize that we are no better than the worst of the sinners. He would have us do what he did when he was on this earth.

Pastor Scotty Smith and popular recording artist Steven Curtis Chapman came out with a refreshing book a few years ago, also the title of one of Chapman's previous releases, *Speechless*.

In it, they describe their journey to authenticity and true spirituality. Regarding the tendency to look down on those popularly defined as sinners, Smith remarks, "When conservative religious people compare themselves with the irreligious, the liberals, and the outwardly immoral, all sense of needing God's grace disappears…But when our hearts are held up to the light of the love demands of God's holy law, we are devastated, we are silenced, and we are speechless. We have nothing to boast in or about, for none of us loves God or man the way the law requires."[4]

The Pharisees thought themselves too holy to mix with sinners. Apparently, they thought they were holier than God was. How about us? How about the New Pharisee within you?

I recall as a staffer with Youth for Christ, I led several home clubs called Campus Life. I remember this kid who started attending one of our clubs. This guy was always going off on tangents in our group discussions, talking about things having to do with demons and Satan, and he had some lifestyle habits that made him a bit unusual. He was suicidal and very depressed. I was very concerned that the group would ignore him. I knew he wouldn't last in the group more than a few meetings if the kids started ignoring him. He asked the group if he could play guitar for us one night. I said he could. So he played. And instead of judging this kid, I watched twenty or more of these teens praise this kid all night. Of course, he came back again and I think he was always early after that. He became a regular, and I was able to share Jesus with him. He didn't give his life to Christ that year, but he was very close by the end of the year. The main thing for me was this: some teenage Christians had every opportunity to reject this young man, but they showed him love instead. I felt so proud of that group. In fact, I told them that their group was the closest thing that I had ever experienced to the early church in the book of Acts.

...we must go after them with the compassion of Christ...

I wish I could say I believed that this was the norm in the current Christian culture. But I fear it is the exception. We cannot love those who are different from us without the love of God. But *with* the love of God, it is easy! Instead of staying away from those people, we must go after them with the compassion of Christ, and along the way, reject every aspect of the New Pharisee in us that wants to judge them.

5

Secular and Sacred

It was late night, about 11 p.m. My co-worker and I were just finishing our cleaning responsibilities in a large office building in downtown St. Paul, Minnesota. Our usual practice was to vacuum all of the rooms in such a way that certain patterns could be seen in the plush carpeting. I guess we did whatever we could to make a normally mundane job interesting. On this night, I was slightly ahead of my friend as I made my way into the next office area. I was emptying trash receptacles while he was bringing up the rear with the vacuum. And then the idea hit me: *hide in the closet and scare him to death!* I devised my plan so that when I heard his vacuum getting close to the closet doors, I would jump out at him and scare about five years off his life! So I hid in the closet. Why is it when you are playing a trick of this nature on someone, you suddenly feel like you have to go to the bathroom? I just held it. I heard my friend's vacuum get-

ting closer and closer as I prepared for the big scare. When I
sensed he was right in front of me, I threw open the closet
doors, jumped right out at him and let out a big "Roooaaaarrg-
ghh!" It was perfect! He shrieked and then kind of stumbled
back against the wall as he dropped his vacuum on the floor. He
jumped around the room like a man walking barefoot on hot
coals! Oh, it was great!

Later that night, we went into the strangest room in the building. It was called the Transcendental Meditation Room. There
were always rancid odors lingering in that room. I think it was
from all of the incense that they used. I realized, as we cleaned
that room every night, that TM had certain things that were set
apart for TM and other things that were common. For instance,
there were praying and meditation trinkets, incense utensils and
other TM paraphernalia (I never understood what all of it was
for), and then there were the usual office items such as desks,
chairs, staplers and computers. I must admit, I always felt weird
about those TM items. They gave me the creeps!

I get a similar feeling every time I walk or drive by a temple
or religious building of a false religion. Something just feels
wrong about certain creations of man that are spuriously viewed
as having divine qualities. Almost every false religion has a certain number of set apart items, and common use items. In the
Christian world, many frequently refer to certain set apart things
as Christian and other more common things are called secular.

Webster's defines secular in this way: "Of or pertaining to
worldly things or to things not regarded as sacred; temporal.
Not relating to or concerned with religion."[1] There really is

nothing wrong with secular things in light of this definition. Most of our daily lives are almost entirely made up of secular things. The silverware we use, the cars we drive, the clothes we wear and the food we eat—these things are secular in that they are not used exclusively for religious purposes.

Paul said, "For whatever you eat and whatever you drink, let it be done to the glory of God." (I Corinthians 10:31) Here, Paul is really repeating the proclamation that the Lord gave to Peter on the roof of Cornelius's house, "Do not call anything impure that God has made clean." (Acts 10:15) God seemed to allow for his progressive revelation to all peoples of the earth for all time by initially making some things unclean so that they would be taught reverence and holiness for the things of God. Eventually, God removed this prohibition and man became increasingly aware that all things God had created were clean. This growing understanding is part of our learning the secrets of the kingdom (2 Corinthians 12:7) as time moved forward on earth.

Secular things are not bad or evil things. They are useful and were used often by Jesus Christ. God wanted Peter to see this so that God's progressive revelation to his people could continue.

I quickly received an education about secular and Christian things after my conversion. Believe it or not, I became a Christian after listening to a TV evangelist. I know it's hard to believe. In any event, I was gloriously saved! And I was so happy! It is impossible to emphasize enough how dramatically I had been set free of so many things by the power of God. I went from a drunken fool to a Jesus freak in a matter of weeks. But even though I was radically saved, I began to struggle because I was not plugged into a church. So, I joined a small congregation not too far from my house. Ironically, my future best friend had just been saved and was at the same church that I began attending. We went to the same college and we both majored in pastoral ministry. It was great to be part of a body. I learned so much about God after only a few months at that church.

But, I also learned that there were things Christians *did* do, and things Christians *did not* do. There were secular people, places, and things, and there were Christian people, places, and things. In the fall of 1984, I began attending this church and a Bible college in the same denomination. At that time, we could not go to theaters to watch movies. But you could throw a cassette in your VCR and watch all the movies you wanted at home! You could not dance. But you could jump up and down and dance in the aisles at the big home sports game! You could not play with face cards. But you could play other card games. You could not go to bars and risk being influenced by alcohol and the presence of sinners. But you could go to wedding receptions. You couldn't drink wine, beer, or any kind of alcohol, but you could drink grape juice and non-alcoholic champagne. You could not listen to any secular pop music, but you could sing *Happy Birthday, Jingle Bells,* and *Auld Lang Syne!* We were taught that the secular things were of this world and therefore not pleasing to the Lord.

A WATERSHED REVELATION

It took several years before I finally figured out this principle: God uses the foolish things of this world to confound the wise.

He uses the ordinary to accomplish the extraordinary. As the church universal, I believe we are still maturing in terms of revelation of the secrets to the kingdom of God. The Reformation was a watershed moment for the progressive revelation of God and his ways to the family of God on the earth. Actually, the Reformation was a major advancement of the restoration of all things. To be sure, the revelation of grace by faith was understood fairly well by the first-century churches. Somehow, many of the first century revelations were lost.

God frequently breaks in through the secular...

Another watershed revelation that was restored in the modern age was the evangelical message. This message simply stated is the message of personal commitment to a personal God who wants an intimate and personal relationship with each individual person he has created. Many believe the outpouring of the Holy Spirit at the dawn of the twentieth century was yet another watershed revelation brought to restoration at this last hour. Obviously, these revelations were never completely wiped out. But for the majority of people throughout history, these revelations were indeed forgotten and avoided.

I mention all of these restored revelations to make this point: are we done yet? Or are there more revelations needed in the church before the restoration of all things has been completed?

Peter, Paul, and Jesus understood that secular and Christian things had no conflict anymore. They understood that God frequently breaks in through the secular and changes it into a divine expression of his power and presence. Jesus changed water into wine. This was his first miracle—making alcohol!

Most of you know that first impressions are very important. I once had a meal with a girl to whom I was attracted. She was beautiful. I was really impressed with her. But, she talked with her mouth full—really full! In fact, she would try to eat a huge bite of food that was almost pouring out of her mouth, and then talk at the same time! I have to admit, my first impression of her turned me off. Oh well. Maybe she learned how to eat since then. She sure was pretty.

First impressions may not tell the real story of someone. But they are all we have to go on. Jesus' first impression to the Jews and Gentiles was to turn water into wine. From reading the text, there is no indication that anyone considered this wrong or hedonistic. Wine was commonplace in that culture and, besides water, it was the primary drink at mealtime. But *drunkenness* was disdained. Also, drinking with sinners was wrong in the eyes of the Pharisees.

I'm not sure if this miracle offended people then as much as it would now. But it is a good example of Jesus' habit of moving within the secular, and making it a platform to display the divine.

GOD'S FLAGSHIP PRINCIPLES

A flagship represents all the ships of a particular fleet. The other ships gather around the flagship, and they all flow in the same direction together. *God's Flagship Principles are major principles around which other supporting principles are found as well.* For example, the principle of justification by grace through faith is one of God's flagship principles. Other supportive principles surround it such as prayer, forgiveness, intimacy, relationships, and evangelism.

You can tell when a principle is one of God's flagship principles because it *steers* the world in a new direction when it is discovered and implemented. People such as Martin Luther, William Tyndale, and John Huss propagated a few of God's flagship principles, scripture alone and grace through faith, and it shook the church, the world, and the future. The world today has been profoundly influenced by these principles. In fact, if we were to try to measure the effects of these two principles on the world today, we could probably not complete it.

God's flagship principle of using the secular to reveal the divine is found throughout the entire Bible. We have mentioned it many times already. Whether the secular includes people (Gentiles), places (Babylon, Samaria), or things (wine, donkeys, spit, fish, bread), God seems to enjoy using what man considers mundane for extraordinary purposes.

Why do you think he does this? Does he just like making man upset? I Corinthians 1: 26–29 says this: "Brothers, think of what you were when you were called. Not many of you were wise by human standards; not many were influential; not many were of noble birth. But God chose the foolish things of the world to shame the wise; God chose the weak things of the world to shame the strong. He chose the lowly things of this world and the despised things—and the things that are not—to nullify the things that are, so that no one may boast before him."

Perhaps we have the reason right there in verse 29: "So that no one may boast before him." Some people may ask why? Is God afraid for someone else to have pride and self-confidence? God is afraid that man will be conceited in the same way that you are afraid that your one-month-old baby will be conceited. You're afraid *for* your baby, not *of* your baby. God is afraid that man will be proud, and thus hurt himself and others! God could snap his little fingers and wipe out the entire Milky Way Galaxy, and not even begin to put forth any effort.

THE PERSON GOD USES

Sometimes we forget with whom we are dealing: God. Have you ever heard someone ask why God stopped the people from building the tower of Babel? I heard one person respond, "Well, the Bible says that God was afraid that if they built the tower, nothing would be impossible for them. So he had to destroy it before man became as powerful as God." (Genesis 11:5–7)

Sounds interesting. That may be tempting to the evil heart in each one of us to think that we could become like God. Sounds strangely familiar too, doesn't it? Do you recall someone else who had similar ambitions? That's right, old Lucifer himself! Satan tempted Adam and Eve with the same thought. "When you eat of it your eyes will be opened, and you will be like God, knowing good and evil." (Genesis 3:5)

It is interesting to note here that Satan did not *lie* to Eve. Adam and Eve *did* become like God in the sense that they now also knew good and evil. But the serpent *deceived* Eve into thinking that this would mean that she would be as powerful, wise, and intelligent as God is. Satan did not *lie* to man in the Garden of Eden; he *deceived* man in the Garden of Eden.

In terms of wisdom and knowledge, sin actually accomplished the opposite of what man thought he would gain by eating from the tree of the knowledge of good and evil. Man became foolish. His knowledge became darkened and, in fact, he was separated from the only one who could make him see and understand. He became blind and lost. But, he did know the difference between good and evil. Satan was right on that point. Of course, Satan knew he was selling man a bogus proposition because he himself had fallen into this same delusion. Sometimes you can technically tell the truth, with intent to deceive, and do much more damage than a bold-faced lie.

The people of Babel were caught in a deception. Yes, together they were accomplishing an incredible feat, building a tower that reached to the heavens! But did that make them greater than God? Again, in the same way that a million ants building a five-inch high anthill makes them greater than us! God was concerned that the people in Babel would become so self-sufficient that they would ignore Him. Why should God be concerned about that? Good question. You see, God wasn't worried that they would learn how to create multiple galaxies. He wasn't even worried that they would learn how to create a new planet, or continent, or country, or city. *He was afraid that they would destroy themselves.*

The more independent we are from God, the more we destroy ourselves, and others. God was worried that they would destroy all the good things he had created for them. Isn't a being that is totally comprised of love like that? God is love! All he wants to do is bless us, love us, and show himself to us. Again, sometimes the greatest blessing is a lesson learned in the crucible.

God loves to use ordinary people to accomplish extraordinary things. God doesn't need supermen or superwomen. God doesn't need your gifts or your talents. He uses people. He uses your gifts and talents. But he doesn't *need* anything or anyone.

DAVID—JUST AN ORDINARY MAN

The principle of using ordinary vessels for spiritual purposes can be seen in the life of David. We read in 1 Samuel 16:23 that "Whenever the spirit from God [evil spirit that God allowed to torment Saul] came upon Saul, David would take his harp and play. Then relief would come to Saul; he would feel better, and the evil spirit would leave him." God used an ordinary harp played by a humble young man to soothe the soul of the king.

Later, we read in 1 Samuel 17 of the account of David's triumph over Goliath. David gives testimony of his faith in God with this declaration to Goliath:

> You come against me with sword, spear, and javelin, but I
> come against you in the name of the Lord Almighty, the God of
> the armies of Israel, whom you have defied. This day the Lord
> will hand you over to me, and I'll strike you down and cut off

your head. Today, I will give the carcasses of the Philistine army to the birds of the air and the beasts of the earth, and the whole world will know that there is a God in Israel. All those gathered here will know that it is not by sword or spear that the Lord saves; for the battle is the Lord's, and he will give all of you into our hands.

You know the story. God gave Goliath into David's hands by using five ordinary stones. God didn't use some holy weapon to kill Goliath. The stones were not dipped in holy water or blessed by the high priest. No, these were just plain stones that David picked up off the ground. God used plain stones thrown by a simple shepherd boy who wasn't even big enough to wear armor!

We could also mention Moses' staff. The very shepherd's staff that Moses used to tend sheep was the instrument by which God did many miracles such as turning it into a serpent, or dipping it into the Red Sea and turning the water into blood. (Exodus 7) It is obvious from Old Testament and New Testament accounts that God regularly uses ordinary things to do his work.

For the one given to hypocrisy, ordinary things are not as attractive as those things that appear to be more holy. The New Pharisee has to create an atmosphere or arena of righteousness in which to operate. Just as she acts in a certain way to appear holy, the New Pharisee also creates a physical environment in which this appearance can be further enhanced. The New Pharisee would never want to appear ordinary or secular because there is nothing of substance on the inside. When the inside is void of any real authenticity or integrity, all you are left with is dressing up the outside to make up the difference.

In other words, if I am trying to create an appearance of holiness to others, I may wear certain clothes, drink certain liquids, and go to certain places that others may interpret as holy or Christian. At the same time, I may also refrain from certain clothes, drinks, and places that others might believe to be unholy.

...the key to the Pharisees' dualistic worldview: they did everything for men to see.

Jesus said this of the Pharisees in Matthew 23:5-7: "Everything they do is done for men to see: They make their phylacteries wide and the tassels on their garments long; they love the place of honor at banquets and the most important seats in the synagogues."

Herein lays the key to the Pharisees' dualistic worldview: they did everything for men to see. They were obsessed with what appeared to be to others. Labeling certain acts as secular and others as righteous created a dualism within the Pharisaical ethic. Their dualistic view of holiness was simply this: the secular was defined as sinful or worldly, while the outward appearance of righteousness was defined as godly and pure. Again, a brief study of the scriptures would indicate that God has made no such separation.

God seems to have made a practice out of making the secular righteous.

So what's the big deal? Is it such a terrible thing to label some things as bad and other things as good? First, let me say that I am not talking about sin here. Of course, breaking the commandments of God is a sin. But what about playing cards, watching movies, dancing, guitars, tattoos, body piercing, and other certain acts? What about actually spending time with sinners?

These days, everyone wears a label. They wear labels that are self-imposed as well as those that have been given to them by others. Labels tend to spawn from this tendency toward outward appearances.

New Pharisees are like the Pharisees of old—they have no inclination to make friends with sinners. They are more comfortable denouncing the deeds done by sinners from afar, or from behind a pulpit. It makes sense, doesn't it? If I denounce a particular act such as getting tattooed, and I have no tattoos, that is a rule by which I can abide. It makes me feel good about myself. I can see the tattoos on other people judge them because I don't have them myself. I make myself feel better or more holy than others, and it begins to create pride within me. But I don't realize I am prideful. I actually *feel* better about myself. I *feel* cleaner before God than the person I have judged.

I love Mexican food. I first realized this when I was in college. One evening, I went to dinner with some minister friends. We went to this classy Mexican restaurant, and ordered some drinks. And then it happened—one of my friends ordered a beer! I thought to myself, what audacity! What nerve! How can this guy sit here and drink alcohol, and call himself a Christian? It really threw me for a loop. I was in a denomination that constantly denounced drinking any alcohol whatsoever. This guy blew my judgmental circuits. But, it also started a process in me of actually deciding what was unclean, and what was clean. It would suppose that this same situation has happened dozens of times since then, and I haven't felt any righteous indignation at all. In fact, sometimes I think I would enjoy a sip of wine or a glass of beer occasionally. Avoiding alcohol or "eating meat sacrificed to idols" may be wise from a leadership point of view. But that is quite different from refraining from things like drinking or dancing because others with a "weaker conscience" believe they are inherently bad in themselves. In that case, refraining from certain things because of the weaknesses of others in a particular cultural issue is recommended by scripture and we should obey such commands, no doubt.

This shift of perception was difficult for me at first because I thought if Christians drink, dance, and wear tattoos, how will the world see that we're different?

A PECULIAR PEOPLE

We are called by God to be different. However, the question is *in which ways?* If we look at the words of Jesus, we see Him constantly challenging people to be different *on the inside!* Love, patience, servant-hood, forgiveness, acceptance, compassion, faith, and peace come from within. These qualities are the result of a dynamic love relationship with Christ. They indeed are the fruit of the Spirit. (Galatians 5:16-26) They are qualities that cannot be faked or acted on the outside. New Pharisees have not made a connection with Christ, have never been born again, or they have become so cold-hearted since their conversion that they no longer remember what relationship with the

Father is like. They try to be different, of course. People will not follow someone who is the same as they are.

New Pharisees wear an outer mask of holiness. Abstaining from tobacco, drink, dance, movies, certain places, and certain people has deceived them into thinking they are more holy for abstaining. New Pharisees pray aloud, wear church clothing, use Christian lingo, spend most of their time at church vying for the honorable seats in the sanctuary, and enjoying the favor of the church leaders. They serve the leaders not because they have servant hearts, but because they are looking to promote themselves. New Pharisees clean the outside of the cup so that others will be impressed and allow them to climb in status and privileges. And yet, the inside remains untouched, neglected, unclean, stale, and dark.

But maybe, just maybe, they are rejecting the religion of the New Pharisee.

No wonder so many complain about the intolerance and hatred of Christians. Maybe they say we are hateful and intolerant because we are!

Christians today are peculiar, all right. Some are downright weird and horrifying! In the name of Christ, too many of us have abused, misused, ignored, maligned, and misinformed this generation. They are sick and tired of Christians walking up to them and telling them they are going to hell. That may be true. But if it is not said in love, we give them no opportunity to choose Christ. We can have all the knowledge in the world, but if we have not love, it profits us nothing. (I Corinthians 13)

We seem to be losing church members out the back doors as fast as they come in the front doors. We think they are rejecting Christianity. But maybe, just maybe, they are rejecting the religion of the New Pharisee. In that case, we should follow their example and reject it as well, and walk out of the door with them. The old wineskins of hypocrisy must be abandoned! They don't work anymore!

In the movie *Bridge Over the River Kwai,* Alec Guinness portrays a British officer captured by the Japanese during World War II. He is commanded to build this great bridge by his captors, so he sets out to build the best bridge he can. Before long, he becomes so obsessed with the bridge that he forgets which side he is on. The British then send a special operations force to blow up the bridge. In the end, the British officer tries to stop the commander of the force, even though they are really on the same side.[2]

I think of this film often when thinking about church structures that have become outdated. Eventually, leaders emerge who seem to have forgotten the original purpose of the structures of which they are in charge. They become obsessed with maintaining the structure more than meeting the needs of people for which that structure was created in the first place. In the end, the New Pharisee opposes the new leaders who have the same goal as the original creators of the original structure. The New Pharisee wants to preserve the old, outdated structures, and ignore new structures.

Christians have held many groups and people responsible for the secularization of society. We have blamed the liberals. We have blamed the government and the law. We have blamed the cults and the occult. We have blamed the humanists and the atheists.

In the Old Testament, the prophets frequently blamed the people of God for the invasion and infiltration of godless paganism. According to many Old Testament passages, those most responsible for the secularization of society are the people of God themselves. It was their disobedience and unbelief that always resulted in this secularization in the first place. When the people of God turn away from their first love, there is no possibility for the pagans to hear and to be influenced towards God and His righteousness. In this vacuum, the influence of paganism grows in strength. Judges 2:1–3 records just such an indictment: "The angel of the Lord went up from Gilgal to Bokim and said, 'I brought you up out of Egypt and led you into the land that I swore to give your forefathers, I said, "I will never break my covenant with you, and you shall not make a covenant with the people of this land, but you shall break down their altars." Yet you have disobeyed me. Why have you done this? Now therefore I tell you that I will not drive them out before you; they will be thorns in your sides and their gods will be a snare to you.'"

It is interesting to note that the word *Bokim* means weepers. The people of the Lord wept when they heard these words. They were convicted to the heart by the Spirit of the Lord as they realized that their disobedience had caused the pagan culture to infiltrate them. The gods of the pagans had become a snare to the Israelites because they had turned away from God and disobeyed him. So what happens to other nations when they turn away from God and disobey Him? Perhaps a similar thing takes place.

What happens when the people of God are *of* the world but not *in* it?

OF THE WORLD, BUT NOT IN IT

One of the oft-repeated axioms Christians say to each other is *be in the world but not of it.* That is right. We should not be *of* the world. We should not do things the world's way, or live by the world's standards. We should be *in* the world. We should not avoid the people God has placed on the earth. We should let our light shine before men to see. We should not hide our light under a bushel. We are to be *in* the world but not *of* it. Great.

But what happens when the people of God are *of* the world but not *in* it? The New Pharisee finds himself in that situation.

1 John 2:15–17 says, "Do not love the world or anything in the world. If anyone loves the world, the love of the Father is not in him. For everything in the world—the cravings of sinful man, the lust of his eyes and the boasting of what he has and does—comes not from the Father but from the world. The world and its desires pass away, but the man who does the will of God lives forever."

Usually when Christians refer to the world, they actually mean certain secular places such as casinos, bars, dance halls, theaters, or malls. A Christian mother tells her son, "Johnny! Be sure to drive the speed limit tonight! Be home by eleven o'clock! And stay away from those worldly places!" Somehow, the world has come to mean certain places instead of what 1 John 2:15–17 discusses.

Notice again what John the Elder is saying. The world is "the cravings of sinful man, the lust of his eyes and the boasting of what he has and does." Do you think these things are limited to what goes on in bars? What about what goes on in our churches today? Can these same motives be in operation within a Christian organization? We all know the answer. We have watched the TV evangelists fall in a melee of hypocrisy, immorality, greed, and arrogance. Many church leaders have been caught up in these things until the spirit of the world completely overtook them. But, you see, they were deceived. They deceived others as well. Avoiding the world by abstaining from places such as bars and dance halls will not isolate us from the spirit of the world.

The world, in this case, is not a *geographical* term; it is a *spiritual* one. The essence of the delineation between that which is secular and that which is sacred is religious hypocrisy. Christians who lack authenticity are largely to blame for the creation and maintenance of this sacred arena that is supposedly removed from the secular arena. They have created a physical image of holiness that they suppose makes them clean. The problem is that the spirit of the world is not a location—it is a condition of the heart. It's like trying to mop your floor with a muddy mop head. You can't clean the floor with a dirty mop.

The dirt is coming from you and not from the floor. In the same way, you can't stay out of the world with a worldly heart.

Many Christian churches today isolate themselves from the world in that they avoid contact with unsaved people. In this spiritual vacuum, they begin to grow in spiritual pride, self-righteousness, fear of man, and materialism. They become *of* the world, though they deceive themselves into thinking they are far from the spirit of the world. These churches eventually operate completely according to the pattern of this world. (Romans 12:1–2)

STRAINING GNATS—SWALLOWING CAMELS

The spirit of the world can be defined as coming from within the motives of the heart. Again, read 1 John 2:15–17. Do you see it? Some of today's fallen Christian leaders avoided worldly places while they are completely infested, infected, and absorbed by the *spirit* of the world. Isn't that what Jesus said the Pharisees did? "You strain out a gnat but swallow a camel" (Matthew 23:24)

New Pharisees construct a sacred world to avoid the secular world—and become even worldlier than the worldly places they avoid. How sad! How pathetic! Now I ask you this question: Are you still trying to stay out of the world or are you trying to keep the world out of you? Jesus said what comes from within us is what defiles us. Therefore, we must remove the worldliness that is within us. When we have learned this, we will be able to live *in* the world and not be *of* it. Until that happens, I fear we will continue to stay *of* the world but not *in* it.

New Pharisees construct a sacred world to avoid the secular world—

Can you think of some gnats we strain and camels we swallow? I thought of a few:

1. We don't listen to secular music, but we gossip about each other.
2. We tithe ten percent, but we spend the other ninety on materialistic cravings.
3. We avoid sinners, but have no love in our hearts for their eternal souls.
4. We don't swear, but with our lips, we tear down the reputations of other people, both fellow Christians as well as non-Christians do.
5. We may not wear tattoos because our bodies are the temple of the Lord, but we eat too much and don't exercise enough.
6. We fast and pray, yet we have no mercy in our hearts for the poor and underprivileged.

Jesus didn't say it was wrong to tithe or fast. But he did say it was wrong to do these and avoid mercy, compassion, and justice.

THE CHURCH IS THE PEOPLE, NOT THE BUILDING

The scripture clearly indicates that God dwells in us as his temple. Each of us is a temple of the living God. The current infatuation with building physical structures in which spiritual acts can take place seems like a return to the temple during Jesus' time. The Pharisees' environment was in the synagogues and the temple. The temple was their turf in which they created a so-called sacred place to come and worship God. Sacred business took place within the walls of the temple or synagogue, while secular business took place outside of the four walls.

An interesting dynamic begins to occur in the people and leadership of which this mindset exists: people spiritually resign and abandon all that is outside of the four walls. They live a secular life when in the secular world and a Christian life when inside the four walls of the church. In many cases, this separation of the outside world from the inside of the church happens as the result of our tendency to place the secular and the sacred into two different categories. The New Pharisee reinforces this dualistic view by rewarding those who act the most Christ-like within the four walls. These rewards come mainly as the result of outward appearances and hypocrisy.

We have two choices: either we can reinforce the sacred/secular dualism that we have erroneously created in the church today or we can begin the process of mentally reuniting the secular with the sacred as it is clearly outlined in scripture. "The earth is the Lords and the fullness thereof." (Psalm 24:1) Let us bring Christ into the secular and sacred until His glory fills *all* of the earth and everything in it!

6

Performance Worship

A Broadway play opened in New York City to rave reviews. The public came out in droves to see this beautifully and expertly crafted romantic drama. Critics said the dialogue was outstanding, the performances by the actors were tremendous, and the story was intelligently scripted. Especially notable were the performances by the leading man and the leading lady. After a month of jam-packed nightly performances, the leading lady began to have feelings for her leading man. After all, at the end of the play, the man promises the woman that he "will always love her with the beat of a thousand hearts." Somewhere along the way, the actress began to fall in love with him. Finally one night, the actress couldn't stand it anymore—she had to find out if her leading man was feeling the same way as she was. She ran up to him after the final performance and pleaded, "I've got to know! Please tell me: Do you love me as much as I love you?"

The actor was quite taken aback. He looked at her for a moment and said, "Where would you get that idea?" She replied, "Well, you tell me every night that you will always love me with the beat of a thousand hearts." The man laughed as he exclaimed, "I don't love you at all! That was just a performance!" She walked away heartbroken.

Just a performance. God said the same thing about Israel in Isaiah 29:13. "These people come near to me with their mouth and honor me with their lips, but their hearts are far from me. Their worship of me is made up only of rules taught by men."

Many times, I think we assume that the people of Israel were not going to the temple or synagogue during times of backsliding and moral compromise. But scripture indicates they *were* attending the synagogue regularly. The problem was *not* that they were coming to worship God. The problem was that they were worshipping God *with their lips,* though their hearts were far from him.

This is scary for many reasons: First, it is quite disconcerting that people would actually be living in immorality and worshipping gods of stone and wood, and then sit in their synagogue and belt out songs to the One True God on the Sabbath. *Doesn't that bother you?* It bothers me that man could be that hardhearted. Secondly, it is scary to me that people would bother to come to worship God at all if their hearts are far from Him. Why *were* they coming? Why *were* they singing? It was obviously *not* because they loved the Lord. Perhaps they did it to be seen by men. The Pharisees did spiritual things to be seen by men. Probably these people were also caught in this same hypocritical spiral downward.

Jesus said of the teachers of the law (Pharisees) in Mark 12:40, "For a show [they] make lengthy prayers. Such men will be punished most severely." It always seems like there are those who pray loudly and long or praise the Lord with great expression, yet they lack any kind of real spiritual authenticity outside of the worship service. Jesus says that their motive is for a show. Again, the word picture of an actor onstage comes to mind. An actor performs for the attention and applause of the other people watching. The Pharisees did the very same kind of thing in the areas of prayer and worship. The praise did not come from their heart. They only honored God with their lips.

TO BE SEEN BY MEN

Jesus characterized the Pharisees in the following passages:

1. "Be careful not to do your acts of righteousness before men, to be seen by them. If you do, you will have no reward from your Father in heaven. So when you give to the needy, do not announce it with trumpets, as the hypocrites do in the synagogues and on the streets, to be honored by men. I tell you the truth; they have received their reward in full. But when you give to the needy, do not let your left hand know what your right hand is doing, so that your giving may be in secret. Then your Father, who sees what is done in secret, will reward you." (Matthew 6:1–4)

2. "And when you pray, do not be like the hypocrites, for they love to pray standing in the synagogues and on the street corners to be seen by men. I tell you the truth; they have received their reward in full. But when you pray, go into your room, close the door, and pray to your Father, who is unseen. Then your Father, who sees what is done in secret, will reward you." (Matthew 6:5–6)

3. "When you fast, do not look somber as the hypocrites do, for they disfigure their faces *to show men* they are fasting. I tell you the truth; they have received their reward in full. But when you fast, put oil on your head and wash your face, so that it will not be obvious to men that you are fasting, but only to your father, who is unseen; and your Father, who sees what is done in secret, will reward you." (Matthew 6:16–18)

4. "Watch out for the teachers of the law. They like to walk around in flowing robes and be greeted in the marketplaces, and have the most important seats in the synagogues and the places of honor at banquets. They devour widow's houses and for a show make lengthy prayers. Such men will be punished most severely." (Mark 12:38–40, Luke 20:46–47)

The Pharisees did everything to be seen by men. Being seen as important, more spiritual, or of greater stature than others was the core desire of the Pharisees. They wanted to be center stage. In the age of celebrity worship, it is easy to understand this hunger to be seen by other people. Many today have a deep yearning to be set-apart from the crowd—to be noticed, recognized, and highly regarded. In fact, all human beings have this desire to an extent. We want respect. We want recognition. We want to be special. Perhaps this desire is not necessarily bad. But Jesus taught that we are to seek this attention from God alone.

In the kingdom of God, everything is turned upside down. If we would seek to be the greatest, then we must be the servant of all. If we seek to gain, then we must lose. If we want to receive, then we must give. If we would live, we must die. If we seek importance, we must associate ourselves with the least important. If we would seek prominence, we must take the lowest place.

There is no other way to avoid the disease of the New Pharisee.

Jesus was a very real threat to the Pharisees for this reason: because He stole the show. He shunned the spotlight himself, and pointed it heavenward to the very glory of the Father! But the Pharisees and teachers of the law would not have it. They chose Esau's bowl of pottage in exchange for their birthright as sons and daughters of the King of Kings and the Lord of Lords! They wanted the glory. They wanted the fame, the applause of others. So they plotted the arrest and crucifixion, even unjustly, of the only just and innocent one.

Today, when there is a decline in the number of converts in our churches, we must seek the glory of God. As the sins within the church match the sins without, we must seek a biblically centered revival of love for God—pleasing him in all we do and say. When we consider the harvest appears whiter than ever, and the opportunities vast, and the intense hunger in the lost for spiritual truth, we must seek the glory of God alone. We cannot afford to lose this generation because of selfish ambition and vainglory.

PRIDE

I have never met a person who claimed he was too humble. Pride is at the core of our old nature. We fight with our old nature every day as Christians. The Spirit-led life is not free from the regular struggle to die to the old nature. Paul said to "Live by the spirit, and you will not gratify the desires of the sinful nature." (Galatians 5:16) This is another way of saying what Jesus commanded, "If anyone would come after me, he must deny himself and take up his cross, and follow me." (Matthew 16:24)

The battle to subdue our pride is not won or lost at a particular time or place. We must constantly put down our egos and our prideful notions about ourselves. Being consumed with selfish ambition and pride is like having parsley between your teeth—everyone can see it except you. Because pride is blind, it cannot see that all that it supposes is illusionary. To be proud is to think of one's self as equal with God. We may not think of it that way at a conscious level. But unconsciously, we feel that we deserve a little fame and applause. We think we should get a little worship occasionally.

Being consumed with selfish ambition and pride is like having parsley between your teeth—

Receiving praise is not necessarily prideful. We should tactfully appreciate the expressions of gratitude of others. Think of an Oscar speech; how often the Academy Award Winning Actor says something like:

> I just want the other actors who were nominated to know that you were all more deserving of this award than I. Thanks to each of you for the great performances you gave this year. I am indebted to _____ and _____, oh and I want to thank _____, _____, and _____ for making this all possible. And I want my parents and spouse to know that I could not have achieved this without them! And my acting coach in second grade—I was a nothing until you came along! And to my bus driver in junior high, I would never have gotten to school if it

weren't for you! And my pet rock, how could I have made it through adolescence without you?

Even the world knows how to shun praise, and deflect to others who are equally deserving.

Many times in the church, we are afraid to deflect the praises of others toward the Lord. We want the respect and recognition. Pride is at the heart of the desire of the New Pharisee to be noticed and recognized. What other root sin could cause us to seek blindly our own accolades and applause in the name of God? What else could have incited the Pharisees to break their own laws and the laws of the Romans in order to kill Jesus of Nazareth? Our own pride keeps us from being contrite and humble.

In the 1980s and 1990s, the me generation was in full swing. Me-ism had to do with seeking pleasure for one's self. It seemed that people became as infants crying out, "Mine! Mine!" But in the twenty-first century, a new *ism* has arrived—*I-ism*.

As me-ism was about *pleasing* one's self, now I-ism is about *worshipping* one's self. Me-ism was about pleasure. I-ism is about worship. It's not that the I generation chisels out a wooden idol in one's own image and bows down; worship has to do with the focus of one's attention, dreams, and adoration. Today, people adore *themselves*. Today, our passion and our devotion are to ourselves. Society of course enforces, enhances, and, to some extent creates this new religion of I-ism. I-ism is fueled by the music we listen to, the images we observe on Internet, TV, and movies, and in the marketing of material goods at every turn. We are being sold the religion of I-ism at a dizzying rate. From the minute we get up until the moment our head hits the pillow, we are saturated with Satan's proposition all this I will give you, if you bow down and worship yourself.

The enemy doesn't need to get you to bow down and worship him, as was proposed to Christ in the desert of temptation. All that the enemy needs to do is to keep you from truly worshipping God. Many are literally making God sick when they continue to attend church services and appear to be worshipping God on the outside, while inwardly they are worshipping themselves.

AWAY WITH YOUR SONGS!

A very disturbing passage regarding singing songs of praise rests in the book of Amos. Amos was neither a prophet, nor the son of a prophet of Israel. (Amos 7:14) He was a shepherd whom God called to deliver his warning to the people of God. Amos began his prophet ministry somewhere around 760 BC. He was one of the prophets who foretold of the captivity of Assyria, which took place in 722 BC. God regularly raised up such prophets during the Old Testament times to call the people back to God and his ways. Unfortunately, most of the prophets had to observe the fulfillment of their declarations of coming wrath on the people of God. Amos rebuked Israel for their wicked deeds and for their deceptive ways, especially their singing and sacrificing to the Lord on the Sabbath while they sinned with great enthusiasm the other six days of the week. Does that sound at all familiar? Let's read Amos 5:21-24: "I hate, I despise your religious feasts; I cannot stand your assemblies.

Even though you bring me burnt offerings and grain offerings, I will not accept them. Though you bring choice fellowship offerings, I will have no regard for them. Away with the noise of your songs! I will not listen to the music of your harps. But let justice roll on like a river, righteousness like a never-failing stream!"

If I could encapsulate the heart of God in terms of our contemporary worship services, I don't think I could have defined it with any more clarity and simplicity than Amos has done here in this passage. What a stark contrast to the current trends in Christendom! Can you imagine Jesus showing up on a Sunday morning as we are singing *Better is One Day in Your Courts! Better is One Day in Your House* and he suddenly exclaims with bellowing force, "Away with the noise of your songs! I will not listen to this anymore!"

Wow! That would certainly be an interesting scene. How would we react? Would we agree with him? I don't think God is displeased with us when we are singing praises to him and worshipping him. But, how many of us are *really worshipping the Lord?* How many churches design worship songs that emotionally move the seeker and help build the financial infrastructure of the organization? I am not saying we've got it all wrong or all right. I *am* saying this passage warrants a serious inspection of our hearts and souls, a searching out of any hidden impurities in the depths of our hearts by the Living God.

A husband got on his knees before his wife one Saturday evening and sang her a beautiful serenade with poetic words and heartfelt adoration. She was thrilled beyond words, and they enjoyed marital intimacy for the evening. The next week, the husband went off to work and spent the afternoons flirting with various secretaries, and in the evenings, he slept with some of them. And then came Saturday: his date night with his wife! He got out his pen, paper, and guitar, and wrote another beautiful love song. Again, he got on his knees and sang to her till her heart leapt. She fell into his arms with tears flowing down her face as she tried to imagine how anyone could love her as much as her husband did. And again, that whole week, the husband flirted and committed adultery. Friday, one of the husband's mistresses called his wife and told her all that her husband was doing. She was angry, devastated, hurt, disillusioned, and bewildered. Saturday, the husband began another serenade when his wife stopped him and sternly announced, "Away with your songs! You don't really love me! You only sing to me when you want me on Saturday nights!"

My question to you and me in the church of Jesus Christ today is this: are we doing the same thing to the Lord on Sunday mornings? We sing songs that declare my only love is you, you are my all in all, and I just want to please you with all my life. I think we should continually be sure we are not just singing these songs as ritual, or for the emotional lift we get from them. Because, if he is not our all in all, and if we do have many other loves than Jesus, and if we really want to please ourselves with all our life, then I would say God feels the same way as that betrayed wife. And it would be better for us not to sing to God *at all.*

Notice what God says he does enjoy in terms of worship: "But let justice roll on like a river, righteousness like a never-failing stream." (Amos 5:24) What can this mean for the contemporary worship leader? How should we be designing worship times that address issues such as justice, righteousness, and compassion? Maybe a better question is this: how should we as Christians apply the songs we sing to the Lord to our daily lives in the workplace and amidst the heathen, lost, and needy?

God is pleased with our worship only inasmuch as it is lived out in our daily lives.

Obviously, seeking justice and promoting righteousness happens *outside* of the corporate worship experience. After all, if you think about it, very little is recorded about Jesus and his disciples experiencing worship together. Rather, the Gospels record mainly Jesus' miracles and teachings. He went about doing good, promoting righteousness, and living that out in his ministry activities. To be sure, he sang the hymns and psalms along with the Jews in the synagogues, but very little of that environment is recorded. I think that is for a reason: God is pleased with our worship only inasmuch as it is lived out in our daily lives.

John Piper offers this definition of true worship in *What Jesus Demands from the World:* "The essence of worship lies in our mind's true vision of God and our spirit's authentic affections for God. This means that whenever we display the worth of God by words or actions that flow from a spirit that treasures him as he really is, we are worshipping in spirit and truth. We may be at work or at home or at church. It doesn't matter. What matters is that we see the glory of God in Jesus (truth), and we treasure him above all else (spirit), and then we overflow by treating others with self-sacrificing love for their good."[1]

My professor at the Christian college I attended used to say, "It's not how high you can jump, but how straight you walk that the Lord is concerned with." In the west, we seem to be increasingly consumed with spin, style and image—it doesn't matter what is real, but only what is perceived by the crowd that we are concerned with. We sell Christianity as if it were a status symbol. Many times, we sing, dance, and perform for others to see how spiritual we are. Maybe we will impress the right leaders and really get in with the inner circle. We want others to admire us for our talents or position. Some of us think we will feel better about ourselves if we are seen up front during prayer or worship.

The bottom line is this: many of us have become carnal Christians. Like the Corinthians of old, we have become enticed by the world, and have taken the biblical model of the church, warped it and maligned it so it facilitates our worldly appetites. We have created a monster made up of programs that burns people out and spits them aside as it moves along apart from the anointing and backing of the Holy Spirit of God. As a result, the general populace feels a cold chill run up their spine every time the word church is mentioned. No longer do folks have a warm feeling when they think of church. Instead, they cringe with discomfort. Why is this? Is it because they have a demon of fear concerning the church? No. It is because all too often the church has become a ravenous organization where only the hypocritical and judgmental can survive.

I realize there are exceptions, and I praise the Lord for that. There are numerous churches popping up that are getting back to the Bible and the principles outlined therein regarding church, community, and life in the Spirit. Many churches that have existed for a long time are getting back to God's design for church and body life as it is written in scripture. I am not here to condemn anyone or anything that is in any shape or form advancing the kingdom of God. However, I think we need to come to grips with the fact that many churches are not operating in the power and presence of the Holy Spirit.

If all you have is the right words and no righteousness, you are singing your worship songs in vain.

WHAT IS WORSHIP?

Worship is acceptable to God only when it is authenticated by a daily life of righteousness, humility, godliness, and service. If all you have is the right words and no righteousness, you are singing your worship songs in vain. When and how are we seeking to bring about justice in the world in which we live? How are we facilitating righteousness in the workplace? In what ways do we allow compassion for others to guide our actions, and the actions of those with and for whom we work? Isn't this also worship?

Amy Grant sang a song years ago that is probably the best definition of worship that I have ever heard: *Mountain Top*

Verse Two

Now praising the Father is a good thing to do
Worship the Trinity in spirit and truth
But if we worshipped all of the time
There would be no one to lead the blind

Chorus

But I'd love to live on a mountaintop
Fellowshipping with the Lord
I'd love to stand on a mountaintop
Where I love to feel my spirit soar
But I've got to come down from the mountaintop
To the people in the valley below
Or they'll never know that they can go to the mountain of the Lord.

Verse 3

Now I am not saying that worship is wrong
But worship is more than just singin' a song
'Cause it's all that you say and everything that you do
It's letting God's Spirit live through you[2]

In fact, you ought to go to your local Christian bookstore and get a copy yourself because it is a great message. (Amy, you're welcome for that free endorsement!) I think Amy hit the nail right on the head in the area of worship. It *is* everything you say and do. Worship is not something you do in a Christian meeting—worship is the constant adoration of the King of Kings and Lord of Lords twenty-four/seven!

As John Fischer points out in *Finding God Where You Least Expect Him,* "Worship is something that can go along with everything else we normally do; in fact, it is what gives everything else meaning. This is what Paul meant when he said to do everything we do to the glory of God. (1 Corinthians 10:31) It's a life, not a worship service, that will make us worshippers. We don't go to church to worship; we go to church because we are already worshippers. And if someone is a true worshipper—which means their whole life is an act of worship—then what happens in church is a very small part of the whole."[3]

Truly, worship is not a portion of a Sunday service; it is the divine presence indwelling the heart, soul, body, and mind of the one who constantly walks with God.

The Pharisees had no such reality of the divine presence within them. They had no real power—no real intimacy with God. Jesus declared to them in Luke 11:42, "Woe to you Pharisees, because you give God a tenth of your mint, rue, and all other kinds of garden herbs, but you neglect justice and the love of God. You should have practiced the latter without leaving the former undone."

I'm sure this obsessive observance of the tithe started out as an innocent inclination to give God a portion of everything. But it sure ended up being a snare to the Pharisees of Jesus' day. They had become so focused on tithing on the faintest possessions, yet failed to offer to Jesus the *more important* offering, their *own lives!* The love of God fills us with compassion for those in need of justice and healing. The love of God motivates us to help the hurting and to bind up the broken-hearted. If we avoid the love of God and justice, God will not accept our tithes.

Some preachers teach that God has to bless you if you tithe. They teach that it is like a spiritual law in the universe to which even God Himself is subservient. But, God is greater than any law He put into effect in the universe! These Pharisees were attentive to tithing on all of their possessions. But they neglected the weightier demands of the law. I have a question for you: do you think God blesses people who do not know him? I think he probably does. But then again, marriage and financial abundance may be interpreted by some as blessings when, in fact, those kind of blessings also come to the wicked and unjust; therefore, even if God did bless someone who did not love him and seek to please him, it would not be an indication of his pleasure with them.

God owns one-hundred percent of us and our finances—

New Pharisees tithe ten percent of the gross income, but avoid any kind of personal responsibility for the state of those around them. New Pharisees tithe in order to receive material blessings when Christ taught that we would receive spiritual blessings for giving God everything we have. New Pharisees act as if the ten percent is the Lord's, while the other ninety is theirs to spend wildly and frivolously. The New Testament teaches that as Christians, God owns one-hundred percent of us and our finances—and we spend whatever he wants us to spend on whatever he tells us.

SATAN WANTS YOUR WORSHIP

Another passage of interest is found in Luke 4:8. Satan tempts Christ by promising all the kingdoms of the earth if Jesus would worship him. Jesus answered, "It is written: 'Worship the Lord your God and serve him only.'" *What a titanic temptation!* The eternal future of the universe hung on that decision. Jesus decided to forgo the immediate reception of the kingdoms of the world and their splendor and glory. He would not bow down to the enemy. Today the enemy prowls about, seeking someone to devour. He wants you and me to worship anything and everything but God. He doesn't need us to become a Satanist or an occultist. All the devil really is after is for you and me to worship other than the Almighty.

Of course, the Pharisees thought that they worshipped God. They sang songs *about* God. In fact, many probably sang songs *to* God. The same was true of the Israelites as we read in the Old Testament. How could the Old Testament prophets accuse the Jews of having hearts that were far from God when they were singing their lungs out to God in the synagogues every week? Jesus repeats this same chord that the Old Testament prophets were hitting when he renounced the Jews for not worshipping God with sincere faith and love.

In John 4, we read the story of the Samaritan woman at the well. Jesus talks with her for a while and then she responds with this interesting bit of information: "Our fathers worshiped on this mountain, but you Jews claim that the place where we must worship is in Jerusalem." (John 4:20)*

---

*It is interesting that Jesus elucidates on this very central theme of His life's message with a Gentile—a woman no less. Regarding Jesus' elevation of the role and status of women during his ministry, it should be pointed out that even though the twelve were all men, it seems that some of the most important moments of his life were saved for the enlightenment of certain women who loved him and followed him. Of course, the most important woman in Jesus' life was his mother Mary. But other women such as Mary, Martha, Mary Magdalene, and the Gentile woman from Samaria had the privilege of being the primary recipients of some of the most powerful revelations Christ ever gave. It seems that the Pharisees had been guilty of the same prejudice that had been the norm in Palestine then. Perhaps sexism is yet another characteristic of the New Pharisee.

Jesus then responds, "A time is coming and now has come when the true worshippers will worship the Father in spirit and truth, for they are the kind of worshippers the Father seeks. God is spirit, and His worshippers must worship in spirit and in truth." (John 4:23–24) Jesus clearly states that worshipping must be done in spirit and in truth if it is to be received by the Father. So, what does that mean to you and me?

What does it mean to worship God in spirit? To find the answer to this, we must look to what the Son of God claimed was the true source of his power. In John 5:19b, Jesus reveals the secret of his miracle ministry: "I tell you the truth, the Son can do nothing by himself; he can do only what he sees his Father doing, because whatever the Father does the Son also does."

We read again in Luke 4:18, as Jesus read from Isaiah 61 in the synagogue at Nazareth, "The Spirit of the Lord is on me, because he has anointed me to preach good news to the poor. He has sent me to proclaim freedom for the prisoners and recovery of sight for the blind, to release the oppressed, to proclaim the year of the Lord's favor." He then said to them all, "Today this scripture is fulfilled in your hearing." Jesus never kept it a secret that every good work he did was by the Holy Spirit and in obedient submission to the Father. Later in the New Testament epistles, we read that the Spirit leads each member of the body of Christ and empowers the believer in all aspects of the Christian life. This includes worship.

Yes. Worship is only truly worship when it is done in the Spirit. Can we worship in the flesh? Once more, we need to read the Old Testament and remind ourselves that the prophets were constantly coming against Israel's tendency to do outward expressions of worship without having a sincere love and devotion and reverence. All too often, like the Pharisees of the first century, they were corrupted with hypocrisy. They worshipped in the flesh. One can do many apparent good works by the flesh. The flesh is not just in operation when we find ourselves doing sensual deeds. Doing things in the flesh also occurs when we use natural human powers and wisdom, or when we rely on our own resources to do God's work. May God help us!

Why would anyone try to do the works and will of God without God's help, leading, power, and anointing?

In this light, we might see that in many of the efforts of the church of today where we are trying to do so many good things, we are merely relying on human wisdom, might and understanding. In other words, we are guilty of doing Christianity *in the flesh!*

Why would anyone try to do the works and will of God without God's help, leading, power, and anointing? Good question. I think most desire to be doing God's work with the same modus operandi as Christ. Christ did only that which the Father lead him to do, and did it all in the power, leading, and anointing of the Holy Spirit. Christ promised those who followed him that they will do even "greater things than these," because he knew (John 14:12) that the Holy Spirit would use Christ as an example of how Christians ought to live and walk each day and hour—even moment by moment. The same is true when it comes to worship.

As we stand, kneel, or sit and sing songs of praise and adoration, we must be constantly in tune with the Lord, and be sure that what we sing is genuine and heartfelt. Worshipping in the flesh occurs when we let our worship become stale, surface-level, shallow, and even boring. But, worshipping in the flesh can also occur when we are excited, and exuberant, and intense in our worship expressions. Of course, there is nothing wrong with singing and dancing our hearts out to God. In fact, we could use a lot more of that in today's services. On the other hand, just because someone is excited or exuberant does not mean she is in tune with God.

Sometimes we come to church and we just want to feel good. There is nothing wrong with feeling good. Sometimes when we come to church, we just get caught up in the music. There is nothing wrong with getting caught up in the music. Sometimes when we come to church, we feel accepted by the others that are there, and there is nothing wrong with being accepted by others.

When our praise is not genuine or sincere, we need to check ourselves immediately. I find myself doing this often. I will be twenty minutes into the song service, and the entire time I was singing praises, my mind was on the project I am working on, or what I will tell my boss tomorrow, or what I want to get done later that day. Sometimes I am just thinking about where to go for lunch after church. These are not bad in and of themselves of course, but worship and praise should be a time where we block everything else out and really *enter in.*

ENTERING INTO THE TABERNACLE

The Old Testament tabernacle is a perfect example of this dynamic of entering into the Lord's presence and laying aside everything else in our thoughts and hearts. As you may recall, God had given Moses more than just ten commandments on Mt. Sinai. He also laid out many specific details for life, conduct, and worship of God's people. The Lord gave Moses exact details for constructing the Tabernacle—fifty cubits (seventy-five feet) wide and one hundred cubits (one hundred fifty feet) long. This structure was the outer court where the Jews were to bring their sacrifices to the Levite priests. The Levites were God's set-apart tribe for the priesthood, and were in charge of leading Israel in worship and sacrificing. The people would bring an animal for sacrificing, and the Levites would check it for defects, and then prepare the sacrifice. In this area were the bronze altar and the basin used in preparation of the sacrifices. (Exodus 25–30)

Within the Tabernacle was another structure called the inner court. The inner court was made up of two parts: the Holy Place, and the Most Holy Place. The Holy Place (fifteen feet wide and thirty feet long) housed the golden table for the bread of the Presence, the golden lamp stand, and the altar of incense. The Most Holy Place (ten feet by ten feet) housed the Ark of the Covenant. Not everyone could enter the Holy Place. Only one man, the High Priest, could enter the Most Holy Place—and that only once a year.

Many have written volumes regarding the teaching ministry of Jesus. He used parables often because, in this way, even the simplest of minds could comprehend the most profound spiritual truths. Conversely, some of the most brilliant minds could not understand because the parable required an element of child-like faith as it is empowered by the revelatory power of the Holy Spirit.

God also used the Tabernacle to help the Israelites understand what it is like to live *in His presence.*

God did the same thing in the old covenant by teaching Israel through very practical and physical expressions. The Tabernacle is like a parable in that sense—God used the Tabernacle to help his children understand his holiness. God also used the Tabernacle to help the Israelites understand what it is like to live *in His presence.*

In Acts 17:28, we find Paul telling a crowd of Greek onlookers, "For in him [God] we live and move and have our being." Paul was trying to get Gentiles in pagan Athens to understand the same thing God wanted Israel to comprehend: that we can and must live *in His presence*. The implication is that we are to God as fish are to water. We cannot live without His presence. We live in the atmosphere of God. Man has no life apart from the Lord.

The Tabernacle teaches us that we must come humbly, with hearts of repentance and sincere devotion. We must worship God in spirit and in truth. If we hope to experience God in the Most Holy Place, we must come on our knees in reverence and true purity of motive and attitude. We must come to him embracing the truth about our condition, our sins, and ourselves. We must worship *in the presence* of God, which is by His Spirit.

We live and walk in the Spirit. We are led by the Spirit. There is no other way in which God accepts our worship but that which is done by his Spirit, and in the light of his truth revealed to us. I confess I would really like to get back to experiencing more of the dynamic presence of God in today's contemporary worship service.

WE ARE MISSING HIS PRESENCE! WE ARE MISSING HIS PRESENCE!

It is the very presence of God that we need to experience. We will find that our pure and sincere worship invites the awesome presence of the Spirit of God. This is the experience I had for the first several years of my Christian life. I regret to say this, but I recall experiencing a power and an awesome presence in worship services ten to fifteen years ago that I have not sensed often since. I am not saying that today's worship is bad. I am just saying that I feel we are too caught up with sugary ditties

telling how neat God is it many times sounds a lot like a pop
service. Every Sunday, we sing to God pop forty songs, and
sometimes that is just what we need and what God needs. I
enjoy today's worship services, don't get me wrong; I just don't
know how much of his presence we can hope to experience until
we move past outer court worship.

The New Pharisee is content to sing out in the outer courts—
still in the camp, even within the tabernacle, but not entering
into the inner court. The New Pharisee can worship outside of
the truth. The New Pharisee is not led by the Spirit of God. The
New Pharisee attempts to show a form of worship, and yet deny
its power. The New Pharisee is not worshipping for the sake of
worshipping God, but for some other reason. The New Pharisee
does not understand the importance or experience of worshipping in the Spirit and by the Spirit, nor does he embrace truth
regardless of personal implications or discomfort.

> **The New Pharisee is content to sing out in the outer courts—**

MODERN WORSHIP TRENDS

Please know that some of what I am about to share is not
meant to tear down or to criticize for the sake of criticizing, but
I think these important principles for worship have some application to worship in the church today.

Have you ever walked out of a worship and praise service and
said to another person, "Wasn't that an awesome worship ser-

vice!" I have. In light of the scriptural truths we have been looking at in this chapter, I wonder what I really mean when I say
such things. Did I mean to say, "Wasn't that an awesome time of
people giving heartfelt praise and worship to God because they
love him so much?" Perhaps I meant something else. Perhaps I
meant to say, "Wasn't that an awesome experience of passionate
songs and energetic dancing?"

Do you see how one does not necessarily equal the other? If
so, then every concert in the local stadium is worshipping God
also. If dancing and singing are all there is to worship, then it is
an external thing, not an internal thing. As we have seen from
the statements of Jesus in the Gospels, it's the internal reality
that he is after.

Many of today's praise and worship songs have an element to
them that is very celebratory—and I thank God for it! Celebration is certainly a vital aspect of our worship. However, we must
not put the cart before the horse. Scriptural accounts of celebration often followed great trials that really pressed the people of
God to believe the Lord would miraculously deliver them. And
when he did, they broke out in spontaneous praise. I have no
problem with celebratory praise in our services, even if it is not
the result of some great deliverance or a wonderful miracle
because God himself is worthy of celebratory praise *just
because of who he is!*

There are those who are not comfortable with songs that
inspire the people to dance, clap, or at the very least shout out to
God. They do not want to get into emotionalism. But there is a

big difference between *emotionalism* and simply displaying *emotion*.

Displaying emotion is a natural part of who God made you and me to be. Showing emotion after a new baby is born, or at a wedding, or a funeral, or at a big sporting event is natural. Showing emotion because of a deep love and appreciation to God for what he is doing and who he is, is not only a good thing and a beautiful thing, it is a command!

Jesus taught that the greatest command was to love the Lord your God with all your heart, all your soul, all your strength, and all your mind. I think we should ask the professional psychologists if it is possible to love someone with that kind of all-consuming passion, and not feel, or even display any emotion. There may be those who feel that kind of deep love for God who display no outward emotion, but I think they would have to have some kind of psychological dysfunction, if not demonic hindrance and oppression.

Sometimes a very moving moment comes unexpectedly after watching a movie or singing a beautiful song, and you just cannot hold back your emotions. God created you to emote naturally—to feel, to express that feeling even if it brings tears, sobbing, shouting, or some other emotive response. God made us in his image. Anyone can read through the Old Testament and see God's emotions on almost every page.

I once did a study on the anger of God in the Old Testament. I found over 3,000 entries in *Strong's Concordance* that listed the phrase "the anger (wrath) of the Lord (God) was kindled." God does get angry. If anger is a sin, then God's got a big problem, but we know that there is such a thing as righteous anger. So it is a good thing to express emotion, and even to allow people opportunities to emote, in the church service.

However...

We come to this whole problem of emotionalism. Emotionalism is an attempt to manipulate and control people, be it ever so slight. Most often, this is done by those who lead the crowd in speaking, singing, or other kinds of performances. I think the heart of what emotionalism really is has to do with the *calculated intentions of the leader.*

If you ever get a chance to speak in front of people, or lead them in singing, or even perform in a dramatic presentation, you will see that it is possible to manipulate people's emotions.

There are many reasons why this is done. For example, many people say that Adolph Hitler was a mesmerizing speaker. His hypnotic abilities literally put an entire nation under a spell to the extent that they were willing to lift their hands high in praise to him and him alone—almost as if he were God! His success in public address was due, in part, to his masterful use of emotionalism. He knew when to bring up the injustices done to the Germans after World War I; he knew when to bring up other nationalities against which many Germans were feeling a growing resentment. He knew how to bring such a swell of grandeur and fantasy to the listener when talking about the possibility of Germany one day being the greatest empire in the world, that literally the entire crowd would lose their composure, fainting, leaping, crying, and shouting praises to Hitler, *"Der Fuhrer!"*

EMOTIONALISM IN THE CHURCH

Much of this is simply due to someone knowing how to use the power of emotionalism to get people to follow him. Cult leaders apply the same techniques. It is very calculated and intentional. Even when a leader applies these techniques some-what subconsciously, the effect is the same.

These same phenomena can happen in preaching. The godly preacher will not resort to such techniques. These techniques do nothing of any lasting value for the listener. When the technique of emotionalism is used in preaching, it is done mainly for the selfish desires of the preacher—most often the preacher hopes to gain a *following,* instead of helping to teach people how to *follow* Christ!

This same is true for the worship service. The worship leader has great influence over what kinds of emotions people may experience in the service. He can choose happy songs if he wants people to express happiness. Or, a worship leader can choose mostly somber songs, and in so doing, can direct many of the crowd to express emotions of sadness or somberness. This is enhanced when instruments are employed in the service, especially in cultures that feature a lot of electronics and ampli-fied sound in their worship services.

Ironically, many times God will use enhancements, media tools, instruments, and even happy and sad songs. Was not David's harp a tool that drove a tormenting evil spirit away from King Saul? I do not mean to suggest that using whatever tools God has given us to enhance what he is doing is wrong. In that sense, words, encouragement, and exhortation could be considered manipulation.

So how does a leader guard against this? How will a preacher or worship leader know when he is employing emotionalism, and when he is being used by God to affect people's emotions? I think it all depends on the heart motives of the leader. If you want to follow the leading of the Holy Spirit, then obey what he puts on your heart, whether obedience leads you to prepare something very encouraging, or something very sobering. Sometimes God wants to sober his people. Sometimes he wants to encourage his people. Sometimes he wants us to be still and know that he is God. Sometimes he wants us to shout out praises to him. It all depends on what he wants.

...when God wants to heal you, to inspire you, to fill you, or to encourage you, I guarantee you will feel some emotions!

God's end goal is not to get a person to emote. The bottom line is, whether you emote at all, God wants you to obey. But when God wants to heal you, to inspire you, to fill you, or to encourage you, I guarantee you will feel some emotions! When I sing songs of encouragement to the people, I surely hope it touches their emotions in the sense that I want them to be inspired, encouraged, light, and joyful, even to the point of shouting if they feel so led. Emotionalism occurs when we want to take people to an emotional place for our own ends.

Having said this, I hope we guard against using emotionalism in our services. Sometimes the popular use of mostly celebratory songs in a service is in itself a case of emotionalism. I think it happens with no ill will or intention of the worship leaders. I think in many cases, it is simply the result of worship leaders using the available trendy worship music. Part of this trend towards utilizing emotionally exhilarating praise songs (I believe many of these songs are truly inspired of God and responsible for a new wave of renewal) has to do with the focus of church leaders, pastors, and elders, mainly in the west, on getting more people into the services. Many church leaders believe that more non-churched people would come if they were made to feel happy and excited as the result of being in their services.

This is not necessarily bad. Once again, it depends on the heart intentions of the leaders themselves. On the one hand, we should do whatever we can to make non-churched people feel comfortable with us, with what communicates to them, and with what will effectively communicate the love of God to them as well as our love as believers for them.

But a fine line is crossed when we start to filter the Holy Spirit's leading in what we teach and preach because we are nervous about people not coming, or leaving.

SEEKER FRIENDLY YET TRUTHFUL

Jesus was a very interesting example in this regard. On the one hand, he was very seeker friendly. He went to where the sinners were. He spent time with them; he no doubt listened to their hurts, their pains, and their fears. He also no doubt listened to their off-color jokes and speech and saw their inappropriate gestures. I am sure he did not condone it. But, surely he *heard* it, and in some manner *tolerated* it.

Walk into a club some evening and try to get the entire crowd to speak appropriately and not use inappropriate stories, jokes, and gestures. Good luck! Not possible. I suppose one could say that Jesus was God so he automatically made the people speak appropriately and made sure no off-color jokes or curses were told in his presence, but I don't think so. I don't think sinners like hanging around someone like that. Of course, as soon as a particular sinner realized they were in the presence of a very holy man, they censored themselves. But, not immediately, and surely not everyone in the crowd did so. Sinners liked being with Jesus. Jesus was as seeker friendly as one could get. In fact, he told stories about agriculture, hardly ever gave sermons directly from the Torah itself when not in the synagogues, preached in the fields and on hills, did miracles that met people's immediate needs, and then followed this up with a scriptural teaching told in a way that made sense to the common people, many of them illiterate.

On the one hand, we need to learn more from Jesus in the area of being seeker friendly. But, this did not mean that he also watered down his message, or the standards of commitment to follow him. Jesus spent all that time and effort being so seeker friendly, and then was willing to let everyone walk away when he spoke cutting truths that pierced the very core of people's souls. In fact, sometimes even the twelve disciples were tempted to leave him, but they stayed, for they had nowhere else to go. Who else had the words of eternal life?

The Pharisees wanted a following. They enjoyed the praises of men, and were not about to let some strange rabbi take this away. The New Pharisee likes the praises of men, and is afraid to say or do anything that would turn them away. The man and woman of God desire to communicate and connect with people, but are willing to speak the truth in love even if people turn away. The New Pharisee is too consumed with selfish goals and building his or her own kingdom. The godly person is mostly consumed with the kingdom of God and eternal rewards for obedience to the truth.

A LIFESTYLE OF WORSHIP

Worship is so much more than a service. As we saw earlier, worship in the Bible is also a lifestyle. True worship will change the way we live, with whom we are willing to associate, where we spend our money, and how we live our lives in the marketplace. True worship cannot happen in our lives without impacting the community in which we live. I also believe that as the world gets smaller, our community has become accessible on a world scale.

One of the most worshipful experiences I have ever had was at Mother Theresa's House of the Dying in Calcutta, India. I had the opportunity to bathe and feed dying people, as well as clean soiled garments and dirty rooms. I once helped a young man eat some food. He was so traumatized that he could not eat. I have no idea what his story was, all I know is that a friend and I had to physically open and close his mouth until his saliva glands began to kick in, and his brain signaled for him to chew and swallow. But we had to do this with each bite. As I sat there holding his jaws, I was not aware of how much better I was than he was. I was not conscious of how much wiser, or more educated, or faster, or more gifted I was than he. Only this one thought hit me as I humbly served him in this way *this is an honor!* I began to feel honored to be the one who could grab the jaws of a dying young man in a diseased and grotesque circumstance. As I served him, I knew I was serving Jesus. I knew I was helping Jesus eat for, "whatever you did for one of the least of these brothers of mine, you did for me." (Matthew 25: 40) In fact, the more I served him, the most amazing thing began to happen,—I saw how ugly *I* was!

Literally, with every bite of this beaten young man, I became more and more disgusted with myself. It was as if serving a dying poor person brought up all the pride, self-respect, arrogance, and self-righteousness buried within my heart. I don't really even know if I saw this hidden in my heart before. But I saw it all that day. With each painful bite that resuscitated this young man, my old man was being humiliated. With each opening of his jaw, the ugliness of my soul was being crushed. It might as well have been my ugliness and unworthiness that he was chewing.

Every time I serve someone in such a way that it puts me in an outwardly uncomfortable and undesirable position, I see my ugliness. I see my desire to be respected, not to look foolish to others, and to avoid public humiliation. How can we retain our pride when we allow the blessing and honor of being outwardly humiliated in serving the poor in humiliating circumstances? We can't. When I experience this humiliation, I come to that place where I no longer care what I look like or who I think I am; I have crossed the line. I have walked over into the territory of the kingdom of God. I have arrived at a place where I now see this poor soul as being greater than I am, and I am now honored to do what was once humiliating.

As I experience humiliation through serving those in need, unconsciously I also acquire true dignity.

Whenever I see this selfish desire to avoid humiliation in myself or others, I am sad, I am angry even because this humiliating stance is worship before the King! We must always take the place of humiliation. One kind of humiliation is damaging to the spirit, but this kind of humiliation does not lead to low self-esteem. Ironically, this kind of humiliation gives me great honor. As I experience humiliation through serving those in need, unconsciously I also acquire true dignity. I am stooping to do what God does. I am stooping to the lifestyle and actions of Christ. And once I am aware of this, I then realize that anyone who does not stoop in similar ways is not worthy of honor in the kingdom. I don't do it for honor's sake, for then I immediately lose my reward. But when I serve for love's sake, I also take on the most honored position—that of a servant of all.

Worship has never been the same for me since. I no longer can feel as proud of who I am and how gifted I am. I realized I was actually lower than that young man back at the House of the Dying, and I think of that young man often.

Perhaps we could all use a little reality check in that way. Perhaps we would see that our accolades, our associations, our awards of what we have accomplished in Christendom are nothing compared to the honor of holding the head of a dying boy as he eats. Perhaps we will begin a new movement into bringing justice to the oppressed, a greater awareness of the needs of the impoverished and disenfranchised in our world. But this must not be only in disconnected fashion. I am changed every time I am directly present as I personally serve the poor, care for the sick person, or feed the hungry person. Not only that, I am changed in this way when I help the lonely, or one who is rich in the things of this world but bankrupt in eternal things, or the mourning, or the abused, or the judged, or the lost, or the bound.

Henri Nouwen explains that when we serve the poor, we are truly serving Christ:

> The poor are the center of the Church. But who are the poor? At first, we might think of people who are not like us: people who live in slums, people who go to soup kitchens, people who sleep on the streets, people in prisons, mental hospitals, and nursing homes. But the poor can be very close. They can be in our own families, churches, or workplaces. Even closer, the poor can be ourselves, who feel unloved, rejected, ignored, or abused. It is precisely when we see and experience poverty— whether far away, close by, or in our own hearts—that we need

to become the Church; that is, hold hands as brothers and sisters, confess our own brokenness and need, forgive one another,
heal one another's wounds, and gather around the table of Jesus
for the breaking of the bread. Thus, as the poor we recognize
Jesus, who became poor for us.[4]

All of this serving of the poor and needy in our world must
happen both indirectly (giving money, praying, attending conferences, etc.) and directly, I believe, for our worship to be
complete.

And then, perhaps our worship experiences and our services
will take on a whole new dimension. Perhaps we will find ourselves on our faces. Perhaps we will find ourselves in corporate
confession that lasts the entire service. Perhaps we will find that
our response to the awesomeness of God is silence. And, perhaps we will jump, leap, and praise with excitement more
wildly expressive than ever before. I hope all of these things
will be part of our worship—and more.

7

Religion or Relationship

A major characteristic of the Pharisees was their propensity to focus on the letter of the law. As Christ declares in Matthew 23:23, "Woe to you, teachers of the law and Pharisees, you hypocrites! You give a tenth of your spices—mint, dill, and cumin. But you have neglected the more important matters of the law—justice, mercy, and faithfulness. You should have practiced the latter, without neglecting the former."

The Pharisees majored on the minors, and minored on the majors. They were so obsessed with obeying the law to the minutest degree, yet they denied the entire intention of that law. Jesus tells the Pharisees that they should have been focused on justice, mercy, and faithfulness with the same tenacity as their focus on tithing. These weightier matters have to do with relationship—our relationship with God. The Pharisees missed that entirely. But then again, God was not really their goal in the first place.

It's like a husband who spends very little time with his wife, and his love for her grows stale to the point that he forgets his anniversary. So in order to make things right, he goes all over town and buys the most expensive flowers, takes his wife to the most expensive restaurant, and buys her the most exotic gift he has ever bought in his life. He may try to show her he cares by doing all these things, but it is too late. He should have been doing the more important things in a relationship all along. He should have been spending more time with her, listening to her, and most probably he would not have forgotten their anniversary (except for the fact that he is still male—so he may have had no hope in that area anyway—smile).

God is all about relationships.

But the same holds true in our relationship with God. More than tithing, more than doing certain religious activities, more than reading the Bible, praying, witnessing and going to church, God wants us to love him intimately. He wants us to do things for the sole purpose of loving him and desiring to obey him because of that love. "God is love. Whoever lives in love lives in God, and God in him." (1 John 4:16) God is all about love. He is full of love and compassion. He is relational. God is a relational person. God is all about relationships. He wants an intimate relationship with you!

God and religion…hmm, there is an interesting dynamic. God only approves of religion that is done out of a love relationship with him. He is not fooled. Just as that brokenhearted spouse is not fooled by the husband who buys her all those things, yet shows her no other affection, God is not fooled by people who perform religious duties, yet do those things for selfish reasons. Doing religious things is not bad. We must obey the clear commands of scripture, but God is only blessed by those religious acts when they are motivated because of a love relationship.

Love is a very powerful motivator. In fact, love has motivated some of the most powerful and amazing acts. The book of Acts is a wonderful example of people who were motivated out of a love relationship with God to accomplish extraordinary things.

Religion is technically not a bad word. But for the sake of argument, for now I will define religion as doing certain activities in hopes of gaining God's favor or pleasure. We cannot do anything to gain God's favor. Through faith in his Son and what he did for us on the cross, we can receive total favor and forgiveness. There is no reason to perform or to earn God's love. He is love. He loves us already. Nothing we can do can gain us favor with God.

Obviously, people perform religious actions in hopes of gaining favor in the eyes of people. The Pharisees were religious so that they looked better in the eyes of men. If the praise of men is what we desire, we won't be concerned with our relationship with God.

Or is it that obvious? Maybe not.

TRADITIONS OF MAN

Many forms of legalism tend to grow with some Christian organizations—churches, ministries, or agencies. It can be very

frustrating and difficult to deal with, especially for those who
have a new wind of the Spirit of God flowing in and through
them. Man's rules and procedures tend to keep a lid on the fresh
new moves and workings of the Holy Spirit. It is humorous in a
tragic sense, because these procedures and rules were probably
initiated to keep and protect the fresh move of the Spirit that
originally created them.

These legalistic rules are much like the traditions of the Pharisees. Jesus found it particularly difficult to deal with the traditions that the Pharisees had adopted in the name of godliness,
obedience, and holiness. We find Jesus confronting the Pharisees
and teachers of the law after eating grain with his disciples on
the Sabbath. In Matthew 12, the Pharisees observed Jesus and
his disciples as they picked the heads of grain for food. They
said, "Look! Your disciples are doing what is unlawful on the
Sabbath." Jesus reminded them that David and his men entered
the house of God and ate the consecrated bread because they
were hungry, even though it was not lawful for them to do. Jesus
added, "If you had known what these words mean, 'I desire
mercy, not sacrifice,' you would not have condemned the innocent. For the Son of Man is Lord of the Sabbath."

**Jesus found it particularly difficult to deal
with the traditions that the Pharisees had
adopted.**

The drama didn't stop there. Later in the same chapter, we
read that the Pharisees were looking for a way to accuse Jesus,

so they asked him in verse ten, "Is it lawful to heal on the Sabbath?" Jesus answered, "If any of you has a sheep and it falls into a pit on the Sabbath, will you not take hold of it and lift it out? How much more valuable is a man than a sheep? Therefore it is lawful to do good on the Sabbath."

And if that weren't enough, he then said to a man with a shriveled hand, "Stretch out your hand." The man stretched out his shriveled hand and it was completely restored. I don't know about you, but that is so exciting to me! Jesus just said, "Stretch it out." And it was made whole. Even more amazing is the response of the Pharisees. Verse 14 says, "But the Pharisees went out and plotted how they might kill Jesus." Can you believe their cold hearts? I would have been exhilarated! But these guys wanted to go kill him.

That is a classic example of what Pharisees are: they are more concerned with their position and rules than they are with people's needs. These blind leaders were willing to commit murder because somebody did something good on the Sabbath! Also, they were threatened by Jesus because here he was showing everyone that God apparently was pleased to do something good on the Sabbath, even though they taught that he wasn't. Jesus' act of obedience was showing their rules and authority to be false. They wanted to kill Jesus because he threatened their spiritual pride and livelihood.

Jesus told them that you could not serve both God and money. Luke characterized the Pharisees this way: "The Pharisees, who loved money, heard all this and were sneering at Jesus. He said to them, 'You are the ones who justify yourselves in the eyes of men, but God knows your hearts.'" (Luke 16:13–15a)

Jesus indeed was a literal threat to their financial advancement. Sometimes we favor traditions because they satisfy our selfish desires. Sometimes we favor religion over relationship for selfish gain. A mark of a Pharisee is the practice of making and abiding by rules and traditions, even though those traditions disagree or contradict scripture. Jesus' healings on the Sabbath offended the Pharisee's traditions—traditions that elevated religion over relationship.

> **A mark of a Pharisee is the practice of making and abiding by rules and traditions...**

MARY OR MARTHA

In Luke 10:38–42, two sisters who lived in a small village had the privilege of hosting Jesus and his disciples. The one sister, Mary, sat at Jesus' feet listening to what he said. But, her sister Martha was distracted by all the preparations that had to be made. Can you relate to this? Notice that Martha was not being distracted by mundane things. She was distracted by preparations that *had to be made.* Many times, we think that our duties and errands of the day have to be completed before we can sit at Jesus' feet.

Martha was upset. She walked to Jesus and said, "Lord, don't you care that my sister has left me to do the work by myself? Tell her to help me!" Martha doesn't even question whether these things need to be done. Of course, they needed to be done! But Jesus responds, "Martha, Martha, you are worried and upset about many things, but only one thing is needed. Mary has chosen what is better, and it will not be taken away from her."

Mary chose relationship over religion. Mary chose what is better—to experience a relationship with Jesus. Jesus comes to us this way every day. You and I can choose either what is better, or we can choose those preparations that have to be made. The interesting thing here is that what Mary chose will not be taken away from her. This, of course, implies that when we choose our preparations or religious duties over sitting at Jesus' feet that will be taken away from us in the sense of losing eternal reward or lasting value.

As I write this today, I realize that I have done exactly what Martha did. I rose early in the morning and came into my office to type this, and I chose not to sit at Jesus' feet this morning. Perhaps this important work that I type right now will be taken from me. I don't know. I know this book is the result of sitting at Jesus' feet on many occasions, so I do not believe that this book is in vain; however, I think I need to go sit at Jesus' feet anyway. *Adieu* for now!

FATHER'S HEART

To understand a relationship with God, we sometimes look to our earthly fathers for insight. That is sometimes a good thing, but for many, their father brings up images of pain, abuse, neglect, or even just anger. For most of us, when we compare God to our father, we are confused because we know our earthly father is a fallible person who didn't always handle things the best way.

We live in a very difficult time. The world continues to change. There is a current moving underneath the surface in our world culture with great force. Ultra-selfishness seems to be the order of the day. People go about having sex with anyone they can, irrespective of the consequences. It seems that more and more children grow up without fathers present in their lives. Children are like athletes—there is no way they can achieve success without training, counsel, encouragement, correction, and guidance from a coach who is committed to them for a period of time.

The theory that children need parents in order to achieve success in this life is under scrutiny and criticism. But, if you apply this same theory to sports, hardly a soul alive would argue with the idea that athletes need coaching. I think this is partly due to spiritual attack from demonic entities in the heavens. Also, it is due to people's loss of the sense of obvious truth because of sin.

Perhaps our relationship (or lack of it) with our earthly fathers has much more impact on our relationship (or lack of it) with God than we know. I have dealt with countless people who struggled to see God as a loving God when they grew up with a father that showed little or no love to them. How can you teach people that God is their heavenly Father when the very word father brings up such negative images and memories? Sometimes, I avoid teaching that God is their Father because of this baggage that so many carry. It is sad because the term father is really a wonderful term.

The cold, hard reality is that all of us, male and female, teach others by our actions every day. We are all a constant living example of what should be, or what should not be in terms of what makes a human being someone that can be trusted. If we live a life of selfishness, we will model selfishness to others. Especially to the younger ones, we have a great responsibility.

In particular, the war against the male is raging with great fervor. Even the technology and socio-economic changes are trying men by fire, as it were. There is no way a man living in this world can be a successful man alone. Men need the influence of other men in order to reach their full potential. Any church that fails to unite men in very practical ways is sure to miss what God has for them as a church, and as individual people.

Men need the influence of other men in order to reach their full potential.

Thank God for godly women! One of the most influential people in my life, especially in my early formative years as a child, was my third-grade Sunday school teacher. Mrs. Arnold was a tremendous soul with a fire in her heart for the things of God, for his word, and for us to know him. I can still see her pointing her old, knuckled finger in the air with absolute authority as she proclaimed the Word of God and encouraged us young boys to live a life pleasing to God. I still remember some of the specific things she said to this day. What a great example to us boys, and how God used her in my life.

The two women that God used the most in my life were my grandmother and my mother. They were both women of prayer and women of humility. They greatly influenced me as a child. My mother was always there to repeat a verse, say a prayer, and give me a reassuring hug. My grandmother is a vibrant, powerful woman of the faith. Through many trials, she has remained true and constant, and somehow always overflowing with hope, joy, and purpose to the rest of her family and to me.

Many women have spiritually impacted me and made a difference in my life. I think in some ways, it is easier for women to relate to God in a relational way. The symbol used many times in the Bible of the church being the bride and the Lord being the bridegroom applies here. Women understand how to be a bride more than men do, of course. Because of this, women naturally know how to relate to God. Men struggle because relationships are generally more difficult for men. I am not sure that it has to be this way. But I think in general, men are not used to seeking relationships with others. However, a man who sets out to disciple others must become better at his relational skills if he hopes to have any disciples that actually like being with him.

PROCESS OF DISCIPLESHIP

Discipleship. It's a word often discussed and even more often misunderstood. To some, it is a series of classes; to others, it is a list of fundamentals of the faith. To Jesus, it was a lifestyle. Jesus called his twelve disciples to be with him. What did it mean to *be with* Jesus?

The Pharisees had disciples. Jesus referred to their followers when he said: "Woe to you, teachers of the law and Pharisees, you hypocrites! You travel over land and sea to win a single convert, and when he becomes one, you make him twice as much a son of hell as you are" Matthew 23:15.

Those who followed the Pharisees' teaching also embraced the same characteristics as the Pharisees. "A student is not above his teacher, but everyone who is fully trained will be just like his teacher." (Luke 6:40) These disciples were indeed followers. They followed not so much in intimate relationship, but more distantly.

This was not unusual. What was unusual was *Jesus' style of discipleship*. He did not call twelve men to believe the same thing he did per se, rather, he called twelve men to live, eat, drink, and walk with him wherever he went. Mark 3:14 says, "He appointed twelve—designating them apostles—that they might be with him."

Jesus called the twelve to be with him. Jesus did not lead them from a distance, but he opened up himself to them. Jesus constantly revealed himself to the apostles—his thoughts, his fears, his struggles, and his need for them, especially in the Garden of Gethsemane. This *being with* his disciples was revolutionary, and still is to this very day. In fact, no other so-called religious founder has been able to duplicate this same relational style. And for good reason: you cannot actually be with your followers and pour all that you are, all that you know, and all that you have received into them without a complete abandonment of personal ambitions and egotistical persuasions. Jesus had no selfish agenda. His only agenda was love.

His only agenda was, and is, love!

Who else has lived their earthly life in this same way? Jesus and his disciples were virtually inseparable. Everywhere Jesus went these men went with him. Everyone knew they were his disciples because they were constantly seen together. That's quite a commitment for those twelve men. Can you imagine yourself and eleven of your friends continually walking around your neighborhood with some strange man? That is complete identification with whomever it is you follow.

His only agenda was, and is, love!

Jesus taught these twelve men what relationships were all about. This same close intimacy is what God is after today. Not only does God want to have the same kind of intimate relationship with you, he wants his people, his church, to know one another with a deep intimacy.

THE RELATIONSHIP OF THE BODY

Paul taught about this intimate relationship that Christian brothers and sisters are to have with each other in 1 Corinthians 12:12–13, "The body is a unit, though it is made up of many parts; and though all its parts are many, they form one body. So it is with Christ. For we were baptized by one Spirit into one body—whether Jews or Greeks, slave or free—and we were all given the one Spirit to drink."

When you think of your body, you think of it as *one*. Your fingers and hands may be unique and have individual characteristics and purpose, but they are still your body—your *one* body! The same is true of our Christian brothers and sisters. We can never be separated because we are one body. When we act as if the other members are not necessary, or perhaps not even desired, we are only hurting ourselves. If your leg receives a lethal wound, your hand may look just fine. But in a few hours, if the leg is not healed, that hand will soon turn white and lose its strength—lose its life. But if you stare at the hand and ignore the wound to your leg, it is conceivable, though not recommended, that you could fool yourself into thinking you're just fine. The hand looks fine. My eyes and ears look fine. Maybe everything is fine. Tomorrow you will be dead if that is your attitude.

We need God in order to care for one another as the body cares for itself. In a very real sense, we cannot truly come into the kind of relationships we were designed for as human beings apart from the divine presence of the Spirit of God. Each and every relationship we have is dependent on first having a relationship with our Creator. If we are in connection and community with God as a person, i.e. a best friend, we then are able to give to others that which we receive from God. This is the miracle of a relationship. Marriage works in this very process. Partners give to each other because each is already receiving their needs from God. God commands us to love him with everything. In turn, he fills us so full that we are amazed we ever thought we needed or wanted anything or anyone else.

Christian singles are often told that they are not complete until they are married. Until they marry their other half, they are hopping around on one leg, unable to be a whole and complete person. The truth is the most successful marriages are those in which both parties were already *complete before they met!* Some of the healthiest couples when they were single were in need of nothing as they lived and breathed in the love and intimacy of the Father who created them and daily poured himself into them.

This is not to say that singleness, even with a vibrant relationship with God, is without its struggles. Most are designed to be married and look forward to the day when that is a reality. But, this doesn't mean we have to grope along and be of no use to God or to others until our wedding day. Singles need to develop a deep relationship with God so that they can be effective now in their most available years. Then, when married, they will be so much happier and healthier as individual people and as a couple. I think more and more people are finding themselves single for this very purpose—God is doing a good work in them and for many, singleness is the process God uses to reveal himself, his ways, his heart, and his purity. Paul encourages us in Philippians 1:6, "He who began a good work in you will carry it on to completion until the day of Christ Jesus."

GOD IS RELATIONAL

Through Jesus Christ, we learn what relationships are all about. Since God is love, a corollary truth is this: God is relationships. Love can only be expressed through a relationship.

Relationships require commitment, patience, truthfulness, faithfulness, loyalty, integrity, and time; therefore, God seeks this out with each and every one of his creation. He created you so that he could express and experience all of this with you. God is a relational God. Anyone who knows God at any level has entered into an intimate relationship with him. In the kingdom of God, we celebrate God with one another in a community of relationships. In the world, there is no room for relationships. Attaining goals is the priority and if relationships get in the way, those relationships are eliminated. The spirit of the world is opposed to relationships and *relational integrity*.

Relational integrity involves our obedience to the Lord in allowing 1 Corinthians to be a natural outpouring from within us to others. I Corinthians speaks of what love really is: "Love is patient, love is kind. It does not envy, it does not boast, it is not proud. It is not rude, it is not self-seeking, it is not easily angered, it keeps no record of wrongs. Love does not delight in evil but rejoices with the truth. It always protects, always trusts, always hopes, always perseveres. Love never fails." (1 Corinthians 13: 4–8a)

I recommend Christians in various organizations including, but not limited to, churches and non-profit groups should keep this passage framed in their main offices. It is the holy *Standards of Conduct* that should be followed in the workplace *and* in the church place. This is relational integrity. Relational integrity is lost when a person begins treating another by lesser standards.

The world today is opposed to God in this way, among many other ways. The world has no time for you unless you can be used by it to achieve its goals. When your contribution is over, the world has no more use for you. You will be consumed by the world after the world has taken from you. People who live according to the world's standards begin taking on these same values. For the fortunate ones who have something to offer this world, they will have a place for a time. But when that time is over, the world will dispose of them without any empathy or concern. That is how the world works.

The world has no time for you unless you can be used by it to achieve its goals.

Unfortunately, the spirit of the world is not just reserved for the greedy business gurus and Wall Street go-getters. The world is also in operation in the organizations run by New Pharisees. New Pharisees, like the Pharisees at the time of Christ, use and abuse, and eventually lose their followers. This is unfortunate for many reasons, perhaps most because New Pharisees stand in the place of God and are modeling to others the characteristics of God. Those who lead will be judged more strictly. "Not many of you should presume to be teachers, my brothers, because you know that we who teach will be judged more strictly." (James 3:1)

If you call yourself a Christian and hope to lead or teach now or in the future, take care that you first develop your relationship with Christ, for those of us who lead and teach will be judged more strictly. I believe we will be judged more strictly because of what we model. We teach with our actions and lifestyle much more than our words. In particular, this generation cares little for what comes out of your mouth until they know what is coming out of your life. It's time for you and me to live lives of *relational integrity!*

My youth minister friend always says, "Kids don't care how much you know until they know how much you care." Very, very true. The same of course goes for adults. A very sad verse in Matthew's Gospel explains, "Because of the increase of wickedness, the love of most will grow cold, but he who stands firm to the end will be saved." (Matthew 24:12)

What a tragic thought. As we look at the increase of wickedness in the world today, we can see that love has grown cold. What every man, woman, and child once longed for they have not received. Even pets need love. How much more do we humans need desperately to be loved, irrespective of our contribution to society or what we can produce for others?

There is no employer loyalty for the worker today. Cold-hearted capitalism is the cause for people's exploration of other kinds of socio-economic systems such as socialism or Marxism, even communism. When capitalism occurs without empathy or compassion for the worker, it becomes a ravenous lion that throws workers around based solely on their contribution. Of course, socialistic concepts also fail for the same reason—someone eventually has to be in charge. Nothing in humankind works unless there are responsibilities and a chain of command. Perhaps many kinds of governments would work

if people truly loved one another and cared at least a little for
those who help a business or an entity succeed. Perhaps capitalism would be the model of the next century if people could
operate according to relational integrity as outlined in 1 Corinthians 13.

I am not advocating a different governmental system for the
free world. I think the Bible seems to support many capitalistic
ideas. But the kingdom of God is more communal than we
might think. In fact, the kingdom of God could be described as
a theocracy, led by a triune deity, bringing together all into one
community, giving each member significance in a democracy,
but governed as a monarchy.

If the world never loves, people need a place that they can go
to find that love. The only place where people can really truly
find love on this planet is the church. Fortunately, the church is
not limited to a building, or denomination or particular organization. It is, was, and always will be made up of people whom
Christ has redeemed and made now the people of God. The
church universal is the people. The church is not a building. In
fact, history seems to suggest that the church is at its best when
it is not able to develop buildings, structure, or organization
because of severe persecutions. The church is the people of God
throughout the world, throughout all time and history. The local
church (*ecclesia*) is a local collection of people called by God to
be in relationship and intimacy, caring for each other as Christ
commands.

The general population doesn't understand this differentiation.
To them, when the word church is mentioned, they think of a

building, structure, or organization. Unfortunately, too many times these places are frequented by the likes of the New Pharisee.

Aye, here is the rub, as Shakespeare would say. Structures and organizations, *which are not the true church,* are made up of many folks *who are part of the true church!* As broken, weak, and less-than-perfect as they may be, these individuals, even those who have a New Pharisee approach may very well be saved and redeemed, yet involved in a building, structure, or Christian organization that others would refer to as working in the church. There is such a thing as an inherently wicked structure. New Pharisees would prefer to leave an evil structure *as is.* Some Christian thinkers would call such a structure an old wineskin. I would agree.

It seems that those of us Christians working in a building, structure, or organization that is in some manner working to advance the Gospel frequently encounter an interesting phenomenon: this phenomenon has to do with the principles of the world becoming a part of how we act and think as people whose cause is not of this world. I don't know if we embrace these principles as the result of working in a structure, or if the structure simply unveils worldly areas that were already there inside of us. The bottom line is this: before long, the New Pharisee seems too often to be very present and in operation, either in part or sometimes even in full.

So in this kind of scenario, a longing and hungry soul comes walking in, looking for life, looking for living water to quench his thirsty soul. It is then that the New Pharisee is ready to judge and ignore, or even worse *refuse* the hungry soul in desperation.

Especially in a Christian organization, a sinner can feel fairly out of place and even outcast. After all, such needy people make New Pharisees feel humble and less than others do. It can harm one's reputation amongst the high and mighty to be seen with a lowly sinner.

When you have organization and structure, you have a construct ripe for the possibility of self-promotion, ladder climbing, greed, judgment, performance, and other fleshly ambitions.

BEING THE *TRUE* CHURCH

Christians all too often resemble the Pharisees of Jesus' day in how they treat sinners. This is a frequent experience by non-churched people. I believe it is part of the reason Christianity wanes in a once Christianized country. Hypocrisy, the lifestyle of the New Pharisees, is nothing more than cold-hearted pride disguised in a nobly religious cloak. But God is not fooled, and neither are they.

We must not be naive to think that the New Pharisee will not peak up his ugly head in each one of us. Rather, the New Pharisee in each of us must be dealt with *on the front end,* so that we can then learn how to prefer one another and build lives of relational integrity both personally and corporately.

You and I may have good intentions. When I ignore a visitor who appears lower than I on the socio-economic ladder, what else could it be but the New Pharisee alive and well in my heart? If you watched me in church, you probably would think I was very kind and outgoing to newcomers. In fact, you might think I have no pride or hypocritical tensions on the inside. But I do.

Nevertheless, once you dethrone the New Pharisee within you, it becomes easier and easier to keep him down the next time. I am one who has to constantly kill the old man, pick up the cross, or crucify the New Pharisee when I come into a group of people and try to be an example of Christ to others. I think many have discovered that once the New Pharisee is crucified, there is a release of love and compassion so strong, perhaps even stronger than the fleshly motivations, and it is as if the Holy Spirit fills you inside and you cannot help but love, care or minister to others.

We can truly say then, "It's not me, but Christ who lives in me." (Galatians 2:20)

The fact is we cannot become mature Christians without the body of Christ. Pastor Tony Evans says, "You cannot develop true intimacy with the Spirit without also developing intimacy with the other members of God's family through loving service to them. You cannot have fellowship with the Spirit if you're out of fellowship with the family. This is a fundamental principle we often miss."[1] Many today claim that they do not need the body in order to be all that God has made them to be. They are sadly mistaken. When churches cease to offer sincere, Spirit-anointed fellowship to others, staying home may be the better choice.

Religion as defined earlier is man's attempt to please God. He does this by performing certain religious actions in hopes that these acts will redeem or justify him. The problem with this, of course, is that certain good deeds do not even get close to the core of the problem inside of us. Sins come from within us.

They come from a wicked and evil heart. Jeremiah 17:9 says, "The heart is deceitful above all things and beyond cure. Who can understand it?" Jeremiah must have had a revelation of what was true, not only of the hearts of the wicked, but his own heart as well. He doesn't say evil people have deceitful hearts. He says the heart is deceitful.

> **When churches cease to offer sincere, Spirit-anointed fellowship to others, staying home may be the better choice.**

This is why Paul could declare that he was the chief of sinners. (1 Timothy 1:15) He wasn't merely trying to be dramatic in order to make a point. He was stating what he knew to be the truth. This is precisely why the Pharisees erred. They thought doing religious things would change the state of their hearts, but it cannot. Only what Christ did on the cross will pay for what I have done and will do. Not only this, Jesus' death and resurrection is the only hope we have for receiving a new heart, a changed heart, the heart of Jesus. Perhaps this is what Jesus meant when he said, "Apart from me, you can do nothing." (John 15:5) Only Christ in us will overthrow the New Pharisee.

I know from my own experience that the heart of Jesus is not only something I received at the moment of salvation, and then I just automatically have his heart from this point on, each day sweeter and closer to God than the day before. Oh how I wish! No, I have found that I must crucify my old man every day, and only then will I find access that day to the heart of Jesus—practically speaking. Religion gets me nowhere in that case. Only a relationship with God will bring me through the process of self-denial and faith on a day-to-day basis.

Religion is therefore inferior to *relationship*. God created us so that he could have a relationship with us. This is the truest meaning of the sacrament of communion. When we take of the bread and wine, we identify with Jesus in a very intimate and relational way; at least, we have the possibility of entering on a deep level in this sacrament. But, if we just take communion and think the taking of it will somehow automatically make us right with God, we miss the true meaning.

Communion brings us to the place on Golgotha Hill, where Christ died so we could know the Father. The cross was the bridge to communion.

This is why *relationship* is superior to *religion*. What God is really after is not for you to earn your own justification, but to enter into relationship with him, and then as result of that intimate relationship he would have you do things in his name out of obedience. The cross is most meaningful in terms of understanding relationship. A brief perusing of the four Gospels provides ample evidence that Jesus was after a relational union with the disciples over and above everything else.

THE WAY OF RELATIONSHIP

Love, as most greatly expressed on the cross, provides for us the way to relationship with God and with others. We love our neighbors as ourselves out of a dynamic relationship with God. Relationships are difficult at times. It is easy to think of ourselves in a righteous and holy manner when we are not in a relationship with anyone. The Pharisees thought they were sinless.

Relationships remove our fantasy notions about life together.

But when God prods me along into developing relationships with others, I enter the playing field, in terms of dying to self, in myriad of ways. Next time you go out to eat with a friend, consider how many opportunities you have over the course of the meal to think of your own needs or wants *first*. Selfishness has a way of coming out of us regarding the choice of meal, place, who pays, letting the other have the bigger piece, better seat, and on it goes. And that's at a meal! What about during actual time with others, serving their needs, listening to them during times of great duress, helping them materially or financially?

Relationships remove our fantasy notions about life together. Relationships are not always easy. Sometimes relationships can test our endurance, patience, and servant attitude. We can't hide the New Pharisee within us in the context of real, authentic relationships with other believers. In fact, authentic relationships with the body are a great preventive measure against the New Pharisee rising up and taking root in each of us. Relationships in the body keep us humble, accountable, and on the cutting edge of what God is doing in us, and what he wants to do through us. Relationships serve as a tool of clarity and reality. We best see ourselves, our strengths, and weaknesses through the encouragement and counsel of the body.

Pharisees do not like relationships. Pride, hypocrisy, and legalism repel relationship. One cannot remain in true relationship with others and retain pride, hypocrisy, and legalistic standards. Sometimes we avoid relationships because we are afraid. Perhaps you are reading this and you realize that you avoid relationships with other believers. This may be because you are giving in to the New Pharisee inside you. On the other hand, you may have been through things in this life that create real fear within you. It is a fearful thing for many to open up and become vulnerable with others.

Nicodemus, a sort of hero figure for me in reference to this topic, most probably had great fears in terms of becoming an authentic person. He most likely never fit in with his Pharisee contemporaries, and longed for something deeper and more meaningful. He was a true seeker. God met his desire. "If you seek me with all your heart, you will find me." (Psalm 119:2, 2 Chronicles 15:2) Nicodemus was never the same after that evening with Jesus. He found himself going out of his way to defend what the Lord was trying to do. Even in Nicodemus' relationships with his fellow Jewish elders, we can see he is trying to encourage them to listen to the words of the Galilean, "Nicodemus, who had gone to Jesus earlier and who was one of their own number asked, 'Does our law condemn anyone without first hearing him to find out what he is doing?' They replied, 'Are you from Galilee too? Look into it,

and you will find that a prophet does not come out of Gali
lee.'" (John 7:50–52)

Nicodemus could not answer their objections. But he knew,
deep down, there was something about this Jesus. Somehow,
Nicodemus' relationship with his fellow elders appears distant
and shallow in comparison to the love and intimacy he sensed in
Christ. Perhaps he was a bit apprehensive about being opened
up before Jesus in this way.

Life is filled with plenty of examples of why we might be
afraid of relationships with others in any kind of intimacy.
Many times, it requires the leader, pastor, or shepherd to lead
the way of relationship, vulnerability, and openness. This
enables the weaker brother or sister to do the same. Many people desire to hear us sing and preach about our wonderful Lord
each Sunday. But then they get to know us and find our Pharisaical manner too difficult to relate to. Again, Pharisees repel relationships. It goes without saying that people may be in the same
place as Gandhi who said, "We love your Christ, but we don't
like your Christians."

Pastor Greg Laurie describes this love that we must have for
each other in *The Upside Down Church:*

> The upside down church is a church that is committed to lov-
> ing at all costs. It is ready to make peace, to promote harmony,
> to lay aside pride and differences. A lot of churches are looking
> around for the right growth plan or the right inner framework.
> And that's great. God's church needs administration and organi-
> zation. But what if we really worked on love? When the world
> peeks in the windows of your church, what does it see? Does it
> see a bunch of people who really love each other? Does it see

unity? Fellowship? Or does the world look in your church and see just another organization or institution where people compete and strive and argue? Do they see us competing to serve or struggling for positions of power? Jesus said, "By this all will know that you are my disciples, if you have love for one another." (John 13:35, NKJV)[2]

These poor, hungry hearts go from place to place, excited about our wonderful Lord, but avoiding us. The painful truth is that these hungry sheep outside the fold have no chance outside of the flock. If we as the body of Christ fail to integrate them into relationship with us, they will most likely fall prey to the wolves, or fall off the cliff and into the ravine. We as the body have the responsibility to get them and bring them in. We are the stronger ones, for we are in relationship with one another as the body; therefore, we must go to them and bring them in. We must not wait for them. We will surely be responsible for their blood if we wait for them to come to us. Jesus went to them. He said that if we would follow him, he would make us fishers of men. (Matthew 4:19)

It will not do merely to sing about Christ, preach about Christ, and teach about Christ, we must live like Christ! St. Francis of Assisi is said to have uttered this oft-quoted phrase, "Always preach the Gospel and if necessary, use words." We must preach Christ with our lives. If not, perhaps it does more harm than good to sing and preach *about* Him.

8

Abusing Spiritual Authority

Another major characteristic of the Pharisees in AD 31 involved the manner in which they handled their authority, or supposed authority, with the Jewish people. Even in the situation we just looked at with Nicodemus and his Pharisaical counterparts, we can see elements of abuse in their tone of voice. They were willing to condemn Jesus without hearing him or giving him a chance to defend himself.

Often New Pharisees do the same in the church. Perhaps a rumor floats around the congregation about someone, and before they have a chance to speak to others or explain their side of the story, they are condemned and judged. This dynamic becomes abusive from an authoritative standpoint when official leadership hands down a punishment of correction based on

one sided evidence or hearsay. Worse, sometimes people are
asked to leave the church, and yet the truth of their circumstances would have at least modified this complete castigation
from the local body of believers.

In 1 Corinthians 5:13, Paul commanded that the church of
Corinth expel an immoral brother from among them. At first,
this injunction seems quite severe; however, later we see grace
and mercy winning out. In 2 Corinthians 2:5, Paul recommended bringing the sinner back into fellowship. This may or
may not be the same man mentioned in 1 Corinthians 5, but it
doesn't really matter. Even in expelling people from the local
body, Paul seems to teach that this expelling is only to last until
the person is genuinely sorry and repentant. As for his brokenness and contrition, it is evident that the time of being out of fellowship has worked its divine purpose. Now this brother
desperately needs the body.

In many churches today, people almost appear joyfully victorious when a person or group is either formally or informally
chastised or asked to leave. Leaders that carry out such expul-
sions must do so with the same heart and intent that Paul reveals
in 2 Corinthians 2.

I have a friend who has been a youth minister to troubled
teens for many years. On occasion, my friend has to discipline
youths who do not behave. Some continue with behaviors that
threaten to damage themselves or others in the group. There are
times when he has to ask a teen not to come back. However,
when he does so, he makes sure that as soon as possible after
that, he stops by their house. He greets them with candy and

flowers, and asks them please to let him take them out for pizza, on him of course! For those of you who fear my friend is a softy, he does not do this to condone their behavior. On the contrary, he explains to them that he does not reject them as people, *only* their behavior.

Strange what occurs after this happens. Most often, my friend develops a very close bond with such teens. The majority of them are back in the group in a few months' time, and many of them get saved and become leaders in his ministry. In the context of youth ministry, often the most disruptive teens can end up being the best adult leaders. This should encourage us adults to treat young people with respect and honor because of who they will one day become in Christ.

PHARISEES AND SPIRITUAL ABUSE

The Pharisees were leaders among the Jews. To be a member of this strict and conservative association, one had to have formal training and hold to certain teachings and lifestyles. Not just anybody could be a Pharisee.

Jeff VanVonderen, speaking at the 1995 *Spiritual Abuse Conference* in Crystal, Minnesota, made the observation that "In order for an act or group of actions to be considered spiritually abusive, they must come from a place of spiritual leadership."[1] In other words, when other Christians slander you, it may be painful and damaging. When a leader or group of leaders slanders you, it is not only damaging, but also spiritually abusive because it comes from a leader who has power to wound others deeply because of his or her place of authority, or supposed authority.

Abuse, by definition, comes from someone who has some kind of power or authority over somebody else. If a thug beats another thug to a pulp, that is not always abuse. Rather, it may possibly be two people trying to inflict pain on each other. But, when a policeman beats a thug to a pulp, it is abusive because that policeman wields greater power and authority. A father beating a child is more often a case of abuse than a sibling beating another sibling.

Pharisees who wield authority and power over others to the point of harming them would in this case be guilty of spiritual abuse. Often, leaders like the Pharisees had no idea they were deeply wounding others. They may not have even cared if they were harming others.

ABUSIVE AUTHORITY

It is interesting to see the increase in books, conferences, and seminars on spiritual abuse from within evangelical churches. The amount of information coming out is extensive. The severity of abuse that many are suffering from churches, and in particular church leadership, is enough to warrant serious analysis at how we are training leaders, what kinds of people we allow to be leaders. Ministry is a relationship-intensive profession. Pastors, by definition, must have relational skills *par excellence* if they are going to be successful at building their people relationally. Consider that we presently train pastors to be skilled in relational ministry by having them read books and write papers for four to eight years in a secluded seminary. Other than homiletics (sermon training), men can make it through most of the seminary training without ever opening their mouths!

Many involved in the study of spiritual abuse have also found that very few churches and denominations have an adequate system in place so spiritually abused people can be tracked and helped. Unfortunately, it is much like the issue of sexual abuse. It is a very sensitive issue that threatens church leaders, and thus their flocks. Most of the time, the abused person must endure his abuse in silence. There is virtually no safe haven for him to go to get insight, counsel, understanding, and healing. I think it would be safe to say that New Pharisees have no idea they are wounding people beneath them. They instead assume that people are too fragile, sensitive, or selfish.

Many abusers were once the abused themselves. Since they have failed to get the healing and counsel they needed, they go along oblivious to the wounds they have suffered. This can and does happen both by accident and on purpose. As awareness of this dynamic of spiritual abuse grows, there needs to be healing and instruction available to both abusers and the abused.

ABUSE BECAUSE OF LACK OF TRAINING

I believe that many times abuse happens because the leader has not been thoroughly trained. People who enter ministry leadership training somehow get the idea that their main job as a leader is to preach, teach, and administrate. Those things are most definitely major portions of the job, but what about relationships? Let the relational stuff happen with volunteers or board members. The problem with this job description is that Jesus was very relational with his disciples. It may be that a leader cannot develop many relationships with the general congregation or community at large, but what about with the staff and lay leaders?

Book knowledge without practical experience is inadequate in almost any field.

Jesus' style was not only to eat and to drink with his staff, but he also lived with them. They went everywhere together. Jesus' style of leadership development is a stark contrast to today's seminary method. I am not against seminaries. They are necessary, but not enough in and of themselves. Book knowledge without practical experience is inadequate in almost any field. For the Christian leader, the process of discipleship should mainly consist of *spiritual leadership training.*

Can you picture trying to train people to be professional basketball players by classroom lectures and reading assignments? Do you think this method would produce world-class basketball players? No way. Many believe a serious revamping of our philosophy of ministry training is in order across the board in all denominations and church networks. If we continue to produce church leaders who are relationally challenged, we will continue to see far too many dysfunctional, abusive, and disillusioned leaders who often leave a trail of beat-up laypeople, staff members, and board members wherever they go.

I am not saying that Bible institutions, training centers and seminaries *produce* this dysfunction. I am saying that they sometimes are not able to *address* it. People who are relationally dysfunctional when they enroll can get through seminary with high marks, and this dysfunctional need could be potentially missed entirely. For those seminaries that require extensive hands on experience and practical involvement, the quality of the training is much greater, of course.

Pastors/shepherds must be advanced in their relational skills by definition.

Even more numerous are people who simply have not learned certain relational skills: when and how to confront, how to deal with people, how to hire and fire Christians with integrity, how, when, and whom to counsel, how to lead someone to Christ, how to lead a small group, how to disciple another person, how to care for and equip a staff of leaders, and leadership development. Pastors/shepherds must be advanced in their relational skills by definition. They are an example to others in their marriage, family, friendships with others, and their relationships with their leaders.

Seminaries and training institutions must lead the way in integrating practical, hands-on training from experienced leaders with studying and acquiring the necessary knowledge. As this occurs at a greater level, I think we will see better-trained and equipped graduates. Also, through relationships, we have the opportunity to discover what a person does best in terms of calling and ministry direction. Within the theological training arena, relationships with a mentor should almost be a prerequisite to an earned degree in any relational ministry field. A new synergy between seminaries and local churches must be developed. Denominational hierarchy must become more responsible in leading leaders, and if need be, correcting, rebuking, and instructing leaders. Then again, denominational hierarchy must do this in the context of relational integrity, or it may do more harm than good. The leader of leaders must be faithful to confront, rebuke, encourage, instruct, listen to, and care for those beneath him or her.

THE PHARISEES ARE GUILTY

Jesus said to the Pharisees "Tie up heavy loads and put them on men's shoulders, but they themselves are not willing to lift a finger to move them." (Matthew 23:4) This indictment speaks of abusive rules and standards put on the Jewish people that even the Pharisees had no intention of following. Did they really think that the people could live according to standards by which they themselves were not able to live? I think some may have been oblivious to this, but I also believe that other Pharisees did this intentionally.

If I can order people to do that which they continually find themselves unable to do, I am then afforded the opportunity to manipulate and control them. If someone tells you that you need to do a certain number of good deeds each week in order to please God, you will work and work, though always come up short, because you want to please God. I know you will try to live up to these standards because if you stop trying altogether, you would have to be willing to endure mockery and judgment by everyone else in that spiritual community.

In that sense, I have you between a rock and a hard place. This is what the cult leaders do. They hand down heavy rules and then live above them so that they appear supernatural, or above the law. The people try to please the cult leader so that they do not receive persecution form the cult.

This abusive trend can also occur in a Christian organization and a church. For example, some churches reward those who tithe a huge amount of their income. The leaders also claim to tithe a huge amount. Now if they truly tithe to that from which they do not also financially benefit, that's another thing. There are those that tell the people they tithe, and really just tithe to themselves, even if it is indirectly. It's not necessarily manipulative to do this if it is done in secret, although I think God would have them also give to a completely separate Christian entity. But, it is manipulative and deceitful to tithe to your own ministry and then tell the congregation to give twenty percent or more to the church because you do—when your twenty percent partially or completely comes back to your own wallet in one form or another.

The Pharisees also neglected to offer justice, mercy, and faithfulness to those over whom they had authority. (Matthew 23:23) Perhaps this is not spiritually abusive, but not to rescue someone is considered a crime in certain situations. To leave the scene of an accident in which you had partial responsibility is a crime. A doctor who fails to heal a patient could be held liable legally and ethically. A policeman who fails to show up during an altercation or mugging could lose his job, and be held responsible for not apprehending the criminal(s).

God holds leaders responsible for the eternal damnation of souls if they fail to show up, in terms of preaching sound doctrine, showing mercy to the sinner, and being actively engaged in helping and healing the oppressed, who are in need of justice and faithfulness. God will hold us responsible for not being faithful to him and to those with whom we come in contact in this life. If God calls you to the mission field, and you deny that call and instead make money as a successful businessperson, woe to you on the Day of Judgment because your disobedience resulted in the spiritual deaths of whomever you may have impacted for Christ!

If God calls you to teach Sunday school to children, and you continually deny the Spirit's prodding, and instead come late to church and leave early so you can get on with your own pursuits in this life, you will be guilty of not helping, healing, teaching, and leading these little ones in the name of Jesus. It may not be abuse in the direct sense, but *neglect can be abusive* in the passive sense.

Jesus prophesied that the Pharisees would pour out abuse of horrifying proportions in Matthew 23:34, "You snakes! You brood of vipers! How will you escape being condemned to hell? Therefore, I am sending you prophets, wise men, and teachers. Some of them you will kill and crucify; others you will flog in your synagogues and pursue from town to town."

How can people claim to be leaders of God, and yet carry out such dastardly deeds? It is because of a darkened heart. Most of the Pharisees were too proud to see what they were doing. They did not see their actions as sinful at all. In fact, their self-righteousness instead made them *livid* at those who accused them of sin. They hated Jesus for this. Ironically, Jesus told them the truth so that they could remove themselves from eternal condemnation, as well as offer them a way to true peace and joy. He was only trying to save them and those they were hurting. And they killed him for it.

Paul himself, as a Pharisee of Pharisees, watched on with approval at the martyrdom of Stephen in Acts 8:1, "And Saul (Paul) was there (at the stoning of Stephen), giving approval to his death."

New Pharisees are consumed with selfish motivations.

Paul claims that his zeal as a Pharisee motivated him to persecute Christians. Philippians 3:6 says, "In regard to the law [I was] a Pharisee; as for zeal, persecuting the church; as for legalistic righteousness, faultless." Perhaps selfish ambition is a great cause of abuse. Obviously, selfishness is the root cause of most all sinful choices. New Pharisees are consumed with selfish motivations, but cannot see that these are at the heart of their abusive actions, words, and thoughts toward other people. Just like Paul, they need supernatural revelation by the Spirit of God to see that they have been guilty of spiritually abusing people.

They also need the supernatural power of God to repent and to receive God's forgiveness.

THE PHARISEE SPIRIT

In John 8:1–11, Jesus rescues an adulterous woman from the murderous hands of the Pharisees. They were getting ready to stone her, for they had caught her in the very act of adultery. The Pharisees explained to Jesus, "In the Law Moses commanded us to stone such women. Now what do you say?" Jesus replied, "If any one of you is without sin, let him be the first to throw a stone at her." One by one, the Pharisees left until only Jesus was left with the woman standing there. Jesus asked, "Woman, where are they? Has no one condemned you?" "No one sir," she said. "Then neither do I condemn you," Jesus declared. "Go now and leave your life of sin."

What a wonderful example of the grace of God! On the other hand, it is also an example of how judgmental and cold-hearted the Pharisees were. In a sense, this amounted to another case of spiritual abuse. Here the Pharisees were once again meting out condemnations because of misinterpretations of the law. Of course, these Pharisees did not think what they were doing was abusive. They had no qualms with killing her right there, in the name of the Law of Moses.

Abusers almost never think that the harsh treatment they inflict on others is abusive. Spiritual abuse, in terms of the abuser, feels the same as righteous judgment in the name of God. Even the disciples had a streak of this running inside their veins. On one occasion, the disciples asked Jesus if they could call down fire from

heaven and torch some sinners in Luke 10:51–56. These particular Samaritans did not receive Jesus and the twelve because they
were headed for Jerusalem. Infuriated, the disciples requested,
"Lord, do you want us to call fire down from heaven to destroy
them?" Funny question, isn't it? I bet we can all relate to situations in which we were tempted to call some fire down on other
people. Jesus rebuked them and said, "You do not know what
kind of spirit you are of, for the son of man did not come to
destroy men's lives, but to save them."

Perhaps some of our righteous anger is merely that of a Pharisaical spirit. Perhaps the New Pharisee in us would rather
destroy people than save them.

**Perhaps some of our righteous anger is merely
that of a Pharisaical spirit.**

THE BLINDNESS OF AUTHORITY

Sometimes it is very difficult to rebuke a leader in a place of
spiritual authority. First, the chain of command in all human
organizations is from the top down, and it almost goes against
the grain of the chain for someone lower to confront or rebuke
someone above him.

Proverbs 9:8b–10a says, "Rebuke a wise man and he will love
you. Instruct a wise man and he will be wiser still; teach a righteous man and he will add to his learning. The fear of the Lord
is the beginning of wisdom." Proverbs 12:15 says, "The way of
a fool seems right to him, but a wise man listens to advice."

Positions of significant authority can be very intoxicating to people, especially to those who have a need for affirmation and respect from others. Often the place of authority shields a person or persons from seeing things as they really are. Sometimes people will disagree with something a leader says or does, and try to speak to him about it. A humble leader will receive this input, if it is valid. But pride would tempt a leader to resist correction from someone with less authority. If this occurs, things can get confusing. Many times, the person in authority will see this attempted correction or counsel as a lack of respect. Instead of receiving a word that brings life and perspective, the person in authority could be tempted to judge the other person's motives, or may even attack the other person in some way. Of course, this assumes the person doing the confronting is operating under the Holy Spirit's anointing, leading, and godly attitude. If not, the correcting is virtually nullified. There is no reason to rebuke another in the wrong spirit. Both parties need at least an equal amount of correcting at that point.

"The road to hell is paved with good intentions." Nice cliché. But is there something to that? I think so. Many have good intentions. Intentions really are not the issue in most cases. For those who spiritually abuse, they may intend to help the person, but in the end, then damage is done. Whether intended or not intended, people can get wounded from Christian leaders. Sometimes spiritually abusive leaders resort to power positioning in order to retain and enforce their authority. Sometimes these leaders prohibit their people from engaging in certain activities as a form of control or manipulation.

Paul spoke of some of these abusive leaders in his letter to the Galatians 4:9–10, 17: "But now that you know God—or rather are known by God—how is it that you are turning back to those weak and miserable principles? Do you wish to be enslaved by them all over again? You are observing special days, months, seasons, and years…Those people (legalistic Judaizers) are zealous to win you over, but for no good. What they want is to alienate you from us, so that you might be zealous for them."

The Judaizers were false brothers who held that the Gentile converts to Christianity had to be circumcised and to obey the Law of Moses. (Galatians 2:4) Paul called these brothers false brothers. They were like the Pharisees. Interesting here that Paul repeats the same warning to the Galatians that Jesus gave to his disciples regarding the Pharisees. Paul says to them in Galatians 5:9, "A little yeast works through the whole batch of dough." This legalistic hypocrisy must have quite a leavening effect. If one of us begins to follow a legalistic teaching, it can eventually spread like leaven to the whole community of believers around us.

POWER CORRUPTS

These Judaizers were engaged in power positioning as they enforced their authority with coercive boasts and threats. They claimed that they were the most obedient ones. Most often, the person who has to remind everyone of his authority usually doesn't have it, at least not internally. Often the most common and perhaps damaging cause of spiritual abuse is the sin of judging. Being judgmental is like a fire that grows out of control in a very short length of time. Being judgmental usually grows in a seedbed of spiritual pride and self-righteousness. Obviously, this major characteristic of the Pharisee is still at work today.

The sin of judging is usually in operation when people gossip and slander. It is this sin of judging that Jesus addressed when he said, "Do not judge, or you too will be judged. For in the same way you judge others, you will be judged, and with the measure you use, it will be measured to you." (Matthew 7:1)

When leaders commit this sin, often they commit spiritual abuse. It is difficult not to as a leader because when you judge someone, you many times carry out certain leadership acts that can be seriously damaging. Sometimes simply ignoring someone under your authority is abusive in itself if it is done constantly and with a heart of indignant silence—as if you as the leader are punishing this person by ignoring her, passing her over, almost treating her as if she has no worth or value to you or to God.

Moreover, when a Christian leader partakes in the sin of judging, the one being judged might find herself outcast from the church community, being falsely accused, receiving prejudiced disciplinary actions and other harms. Just as the Pharisees cast out the sinners from their presence, the New Pharisee in us would have us cast away the sinner or weak brother or sister in the name of righteousness.

The leader who wishes to remove the New Pharisee within him so that he can cease such judging must take on the same position that Jesus Christ took—that of a servant. Jesus washed his disciples' feet, and then he explained to them, "Now that I, your Lord and teacher, have washed your feet, you also should wash another's feet. I have set you an example that you should do as I have done for you. I tell you the truth, no servant is greater than his master." (John 13:14–16a)

As a servant, we no longer elevate ourselves regarding our fellow brothers and sisters. Taking the *lowest place,* we can then be in the same dimension as Jesus. We can take up, and take on, the attitude of Jesus Christ:

> Your attitude should be the same as that of Christ Jesus: Who, being in very nature God, did not consider equality with God something to be grasped, but made himself nothing, taking the very nature of a servant, being made in human likeness. And being found in appearance as a man, he humbled himself and became obedient to death—even death on a cross! Therefore, God exalted him to the highest place and gave him the name that is above every name, that at the name of Jesus every knee should bow, in heaven and on earth and under the earth, and every tongue confess that Jesus Christ is Lord, to the glory of God the Father. (Philippians 2:5–11)

Are we above our Lord and Master?

HERE COMES THE JUDGE!

Amen! Isn't it amazing that the Creator of the universe humbled himself to the point of dying on the cross—the cross of wood that he created? (Colossians 1:16) How can we raise ourselves up over our brothers and sisters in terms of our attitude and actions when Jesus took the lowest place? Are we above our

Lord and Master? No. If we embrace a superior attitude, we blindly embrace pride and hypocrisy. The sin of judging blinds the person who judges, and therefore creates in her hypocrisy. Since the worst of all sins *is* judging, hypocrisy is birthed at that moment because we fool ourselves by thinking we are any better. We are not.

Dan Kimble, in *Emerging Church,* talks about a recent survey he and some of his assistants took on the University of California Santa Cruz campus. They asked students two questions:

1. What comes to your mind when you hear the name Jesus?
2. What comes to your mind when you hear the word Christian?

The students were incredibly positive when answering the first question. "Jesus was beautiful." "I want to be like Jesus." "Jesus was a liberator of women." "I'm all about Jesus." "I want to be a follower of Jesus." But the answers from these same students to the second question were heartbreaking. "Christians have taken the teachings of Jesus and really messed them up." "I would want to be a Christian, but I have never met one." "Christians are dogmatic and closed-minded." "Christians are supposed to be loving, but I have never met any that are." "Christians should be taken outside and shot." Kimble explains that they are finding "younger generations today are wide open to Jesus—but it is Christians who are often the stumbling block to them."[2]

Just like in Jesus' day, people in general do not seem to have a problem with Jesus. They just don't like Christians, in particular those who deny Christ with their lifestyle and actions. In that sense, they stand alongside of God himself and together with him; they judge (in the righteous sense) the hypocrisy of the New Pharisee. The religion of the New Pharisee has to go.

The most damning denunciation of the Pharisees is found in John 8:44, "You belong to your father, the devil, and you want to carry out your father's desire. He was a murderer from the beginning, not holding on to the truth, for there is no truth in him."

Jesus called the Pharisees the sons of the devil. Can you comprehend this scandal? The leaders of the chosen people of God are the sons of the devil. The people who avoid adulterous affairs, and stay in church and study the scriptures and observe religious acts are the sons of the devil. I would think to myself if they are the sons of the devil, what in the world must I be?

...the Pharisees kept seekers of God out and away from the synagogues.

At surface level, it seems exaggerated at least to call the Pharisees the sons of the devil. But after looking into the heart of the matter, and considering the interior state of the Pharisees, this accusation starts to make sense. Jesus no doubt sounded crazy for making such an accusation. But he was right, of course. They really were of their father the devil and they really did keep the will of Satan alive and well in their arena of influence. Pastor Stuart Briscoe says, "Good people, with best of intentions, can end up doing the devil's work for him."[3]

The abuse lies in the fact that the Pharisees kept seekers of God out and away from the synagogues. They pushed the people away. In a sense, they spiritually murdered people.

It is time for people once again to count the cost, and renew their commitment to Christ. In fact, perhaps right now you and I should get on our knees and repent of living like Pharisees, and not living like Jesus. Perhaps leaders should lead the way in this, for truly vulnerability and honesty from the pulpits will result in the same authentic self-disclosure in the pew. Perhaps the church all across the globe should take a month and do nothing but come together for quiet reflection, repentance, and corporate confessions of a hypocritical life lived for the admiration of others, and not solely for the glory of God.

9

Revivals and Pharisees

Revival is a popular word these days. Everybody likes a good revival. Some types of revivals immediately come to mind such as a revival of certain styles of music, revival of a classic theatrical production, revival of specific foods, architecture, literature—you can insert pretty much anything, and there could most likely be a revival of it from time to time. A few years ago, I was enjoying a day at an amusement park with some friends when we decided to watch a musical revival of music from the 1960s. It was a fabulous show. I'm not quite convinced that this one show actually created a worldwide revival. But I will say this: everyone in that little auditorium was definitely excited to hear '60s music again!

I think of that performance often when I think of the word revival. A revival really has no meaning outside of the particular subject to which you are referring. It is similar to people saying they have been born again. They could mean they have been reborn through faith in Jesus Christ and that their spirits have come alive. On the other hand, perhaps they just are saying that something new and exciting has happened in their life and they are glad for the change. People often say, "Oh, I feel like a brand new person." They are not necessarily saying that they have become a Christian. They just feel different in a pleasant sort of way.

When you ask zealous Christians what they pray for in terms of the impact of the church and on society, many will reply, "I am praying for revival." What do they really mean? What are they really asking God to do?

SIGNS AND WONDERS

Sometimes we forget that we define terms many times from a traditional point of view or mindset that has passed down through generations and as a result, the term loses its original intent, and many times becomes inaccurate, and even sometimes completely ambiguous.

As twenty-first century Christians, we often look to the past few centuries of church history to define and qualify the methods we use and sometimes even the theological basis for those methods more than we look to the Word of God and the leading of the Holy Spirit. We are tempted and often give in to the temptation to base our hopes and trust on the traditions of the recent past. This happens with pursuit of revival.

We must realize that the very mention of the term *revival* brings an immediate sense or understanding to our minds. Some of you may have thoughts of miracles and healings, hearkening back to the healing revivals of the twentieth century. Some of you may have had visions of people falling under the power of the Spirit of God. Others may think of unusual occurrences such as swinging from chandeliers, rolling in the aisles, barking, leaping, and perhaps even snake handling. Still others define revival in terms of evangelism and masses coming to the front of the stage in huge stadiums.

Wanting and praying for fantastic miracles is not wrong. In fact, Jesus promised us, as his disciples, that we would do these things in his name. Mark 16:17–18 says, "And these things will accompany those who believe: In my name they will drive out demons; they will speak in new tongues; they will pick up snakes with their hands; and when they drink deadly poison, it will not hurt them at all; they will place their hands on sick people, and they will get well."

There is nothing wrong with praying for miracles. Jesus told us to ask for great things. Matthew 17:20 says, "I tell you the truth, if you have faith as a mustard seed, you can say to this mountain, 'Move from here to there' and it will move. Nothing will be impossible for you." I think the disciples were inclined to believe Jesus was speaking in literal terms. After all, months earlier he calmed a wicked storm with one word!

Clearly, God wants his children to pray for and expect miracles. But, first things first.

CART BEFORE THE HORSE

I once bought a model car, opened the package, and expected to play with it immediately. I was disappointed when I realized it was in about a hundred pieces. I needed to go to the store and by glue, paint, and masking tape and then actually build the car. Once I built the model car, I was able to play with it.

Before we do the miraculous, we need to be in proper order with God relationally.

The old cliché holds true here. We sometimes put the cart before the horse when it comes to praying for miracles, signs, and wonders. We treat the things of God like that plastic model car. We want to run out there and do miracles right away. But, Jesus didn't promise miracles to just anybody. Before we do the miraculous, we need to be in proper order with God relationally.

Paul said to the saints in Philippi, "I consider everything a loss compared to the surpassing greatness of knowing Christ Jesus my Lord...I consider them rubbish, that I may gain Christ." (Phil 3:8)

Paul had things right. His priorities were in order. He was in right relationship with God. *The Westminster Confession* stated it this way: the purpose of life is to love God and enjoy him forever. I once led a youth ministry that had this oft-quoted purpose statement, "To know God and make him known." Matthew 6:33 says, "But seek first the kingdom of God and His righteousness, and all these things will be added unto you."

The counsel of the Word of God is to love the Lord your God with *all* you heart, soul, mind, and strength. This is the greatest commandment. When we love the Lord with all our hearts, we are now in position to ask for, and do the miraculous.

An old country preacher was reading through the book of Acts. He cried out to God one day, "Oh God! Where are the miracles of Paul? Where are the signs and wonders of Peter?" The Lord replied, "Where are the Pauls? Where are the Peters?" Apparently, God suggested, at least to that country preacher, that the quality of a person's faith and relationship with God has something to do with the ability to see and do the miraculous.

The horse—in this case our first love being Christ and only Christ—has to come before the cart—seeing the miracles, signs, and wonders. However, I think we should consider some miraculous happenings of a few hundred years ago before we suggest that making things right with God relationally is not all that miraculous.

GREAT AWAKENINGS

There have been numerous renewals of faith and passion for Christ and his kingdom throughout history, many would call them revivals. Whatever you call them, they have made great contributions to the world. The most well known interpretation of the term revival in Christendom is perhaps also the most biblical. 2 Chronicles 7:14 provides a good recipe I believe, for revival among God's people: "If My people, who are called by name, will humble themselves and pray and seek my face and turn from their wicked ways, then will I hear from heaven and will forgive their sin and heal their land."

I realize that some Bible scholars are not comfortable for this recipe for a number of reasons. First, this was a promise made to Solomon regarding God's chosen people, primarily. Interpretations of promises or prophecies should be made carefully. But, who could argue that repentance is not a condition required by God if we hope to receive personal forgiveness and restoration, and even deliverance from the things that bind us? Second, scholars would remind us that this promise is a very personal and specific promise made to Israel after they built and dedicated the temple under the old covenant.

On the other hand, the same Spirit of God moved in similar fashion in the ministry of Jesus, the apostles, as well as Paul. It is not only in the Old Testament that God makes specific promises to people and reveals himself in extraordinary ways. The book of Acts is testament to that fact. The Old Testament has great value for understanding God's ways and his character. God used nations to punish other nations in the Old Testament. Some Christian historians who happen to believe in God's justice will tell us that it appears that this trend has continued throughout history and up to our present times. Perhaps God is always at work in this earth that he created, though he is not engaged in ruling this present world in the fullest sense, at least not yet.

In any event, the character of God expressed throughout the entirety of scripture would indicate that 2 Chronicles 7:14 is repeated in various ways time and time again. Therefore, it doesn't really matter that this particular instance was intended for the people of Israel under Solomon's rule. God calls people everywhere to repent of their evil deeds. Period!

REPENT OR ELSE!

Think about the word "repentance". When you read this word, perhaps images of John the Baptist come to your mind. He was the crazy man with grasshopper legs between his teeth and animal skins for clothing, running all over the desert, calling people to repent. He was a later version of the prophet Jonah. The difference was, everyone repented at Jonah's preaching. But for John, many did not repent. The elders and Pharisees acted as if they repented, but only did so because they knew the people liked John. It was a good political move on their part. John blasted them for this as he cried out at them, "You brood of vipers! Who warned you to flee from the coming wrath? Produce fruit in keeping with repentance. And do not think you can say to yourselves, 'We have Abraham as our father.' I tell you that out of these stones God can raise up children for Abraham. The ax is already laid at the root of the trees, and every tree that does not produce good fruit will be cut down, and thrown into the fire." (Matthew 3:7–10)

John had apparently seen through the exterior games of the Pharisees and Sadducees in the same way that Jesus did. They had not fooled him. Jesus picked up this same message at the outset of his ministry. Matthew 4:17 says, "From that time on Jesus began to preach, 'Repent, for the kingdom of heaven is near.'"

The message of repentance was, in itself, the good news in this sense: the kingdom of heaven is near. The Gospel is good news. That good news is that salvation is available to all who would come and believe. The command to repent and believe the Gospel was also repeated in Mark 1:15, "The kingdom of God is near. Repent and believe the good news." And again, the apostles continued to preach this even after the outpouring of the Holy Spirit on the day of Pentecost in Acts 2:38, "Peter replied, 'Repent and be baptized, every one of you, in the name of Jesus Christ for the forgiveness of your sins.'"

Also, Peter said to the people in Acts 3:19, "Repent, then, and turn to God, so that your sins may be wiped out."

Some people today teach that all of our sins were already wiped out by Christ's death on the cross. If that is true, then why do people need to repent? Why did Peter tell the people that they needed to repent and turn to God in order for their sins to be wiped out?

Again, from looking at everything from the context of relationship, it becomes easy to see the truth about this idea of repentance.

If I steal your coat and we are good friends, should you not immediately forgive me? Yes. You must immediately forgive me. But in terms of relationship, would everything be okay between us? No. But didn't you forgive me? Yes, but now our relationship has been broken. You have forgiven me, but our relationship cannot continue until I ask for forgiveness and make the wrong right.

In terms of forgiveness, I must forgive you regardless of what you do, but in terms of relationship, I must do something to make it right. In the relational sense, you cannot love God and follow him unless you continually keep accounts clean with him. Repentance is necessary for restored relationship. Repentance is necessary for obedience to God.

REPENTANCE CREATES REVIVAL

God always wants to renew us, revive us, awake us, and move us! It is we, his people, who have a problem with wanting all this. Many times, we are so far from God that we have to pass through many years of breaking and purifying before we are actually ready for revival.

Charles Finney, in his masterpiece *Lectures on Revival,* says this about our responsibility regarding revival:

> The fact is that Christians are more to blame for not being revived than sinners are for not being converted. And if they aren't awakened, they can rest assured that God will come to them with judgment. God often visited the people of Israel with judgments because his prophets had called and they refused to repent and to be revived! How often has God cursed churches, even whole denominations, because they would not wake up and seek the Lord praying, "Will you not revive us again that your people may rejoice in you?"[1]

Finney defined revival this way: "Revival is the renewal of the first love of Christians, resulting in the awakening and conversion of sinners to God. A revival of true Christianity arouses, quickens, and reclaims the backslidden church and awakens all classes, insuring attention to the claims of God. Revival presupposes that the church is mired in a backslidden state."[2]

Finney goes on to include the following steps as being part of an authentic revival:

1. A revival always includes Christians being convicted of their sins.
2. Backslidden Christians repent.
3. The faith of Christians is renewed.
4. Revival breaks the power of the world and sin over Christians.
5. When churches awake and reform in this way, reformation and salvation of sinners follow, moving through the same states of conviction, repentance, and reformation.[3]

REVIVAL OF RELATIONSHIP

When we look at what scripture claims God is after in terms of the purpose of men and women, there is no way we can miss the fact that he loves us. God loves us and desires relationship. God never leaves man, but man frequently leaves God to pursue other things, be they ever so good or godly. Revival may be the will of God, or it may not be—it depends on what we mean specifically when we pray for revival.

Henry Blackaby defines biblical revival in *Chosen to be God's Prophet:*

> When God's people realized they had departed from God and then returned to Him, God brought revival. Revival is simply God returning to his people in all His fullness and power, and demonstrating His presence in His people to a watching world. This is our greatest need today. But most of God's people do not believe they have moved away from Him. Their religious activ-

ity continues, causing them to believe they have not departed from Him. But too often when the covenant [i.e., the clear commands of Christ] are placed alongside their lives, their families, or their churches, it is very clear that they are now living a long way from the expectations of God. Consequently, they are content to live without the manifest presence of God. Because of this absence of the mighty power of God in and through His people, the world has little or no encounter with God.[4]

The only revival God is after is a revival of relationship between himself and the people he has created! He created men and women to know him and love him. If that is the main purpose of man's existence, and that is mainly all God is after in terms of why he created us, then why would we seek anything else? It is not wrong to desire a revival of miracles, signs, and wonders. It is not wrong to pray for a revival of evangelism and outpouring of the Spirit of God. Neither is it wrong to pray for a revival of cities and nations turning away from sins. But all these revivals are subservient to this one end, that God and man are reunited in a relationship of love and intimacy.

The only revival God is after is a revival of relationship between himself and the people he has created!

THAT IS WHY HE CREATED US!

He wants a white-hot love relationship with us! God wants to heal, deliver, fill, restore, and much more! But he does these things as they relate to relationship with men and women. True biblical revival has occurred many times throughout history. In fact, when we repent, a revival takes place in us! But often, a revival comes and goes in stages.

THREE STAGES OF REVIVAL

You've probably heard of these three stages. The first stage of revival is commonly known as the *fire stage*. In this stage, the leaders are pioneers of a new move of the Spirit of God. These early leaders are characterized as being passionate for the work of God and restoring the original intentions of Christ's commands to go and make disciples. (Matthew 28:18–20) They serve as trailblazers for a new way, which others can follow. The sacrifice and even persecutions that these pioneers endure is used by God to purify them and mature them. So they follow the Spirit of God and in most cases, they build new wineskins in which the new wine can be preserved and used. Sometimes buildings and structures are the housing for these new fires. But more than this, the structures and organizations that house the move of God eventually result in the blessing of many.

The second stage of revival has now begun at this point as the structures have been erected, and now a second generation of leaders takes over. The second generation inherits the blessings from the obedience of the first generation. This is known as the *embers stage*. When fires turn to embers, there is still heat of passion and faith, but it has cooled considerably. This is perhaps the most dangerous of the stages because it is in this stage that a person can actually be the most comfortable and selfish. The blessings of the first stage are enjoyed by the second generation as they coast along, unaware of the precarious situation they are in. They are the ones which the Spirit of Christ addressed in Revelation 3:16, "So, because you are lukewarm—neither hot nor cold—I am about to spit you out of my mouth." Sometimes the second generation is able to renew the fires of that first love for Jesus. But most often, they turn from Jesus and waste away all that God has provided for them and for those to whom they were to pass Christ along.

Then the third generation comes along. The passion of the first generation is long gone. The fire has gone from embers to what it is now *ashes*. The movement of God in the first generation is celebrated, but not repeated or emulated. In this last stage, people are cold, dead, and completely unaware of the spiritual condition of their own hearts. A new move of God is needed. Most often, it will take a new generation to rise up and pioneer this new move of God somewhere else.

Each stage of revival usually has certain kinds of leaders. The leaders in the first generation have been tried by fire through the difficulties experienced as they pioneered a new move of God. These leaders have been trained and purified by tribulation and persecutions both great and small. In a sense, this trying as the result of pioneering is itself the prevention against stagnation and backsliding. If only each generation could pioneer something new, perhaps we would not continue to see so many cycles of these three stages of revival.

The leaders of second-generation revivals are usually characterized by gifted, passionate people, and perhaps chosen by the first generation. They hope to see the movement continue and grow—of course, this is their job. Which of us would not want

this? But often, they lead a people who are no longer on the cut
ting edge of birthing a new thing. A very sad statement is found
in Judges 2:10 that depicts this tendency to forget the Lord and
his ways: "After that whole generation had been gathered to
their fathers, another generation grew up, who knew neither the
Lord nor what he had done for Israel."

Every generation must rediscover God for itself. You cannot
inherit a relationship with God. Each generation must approach
God on his terms and seek him, so that it can find him. To those who
seek him with all their hearts, he will make himself known to them.

Every generation must rediscover God for itself.

Perhaps the first generation forgets to pass along the knowledge of God and his ways. Psalm 71:18 says, "Even when I am
old and gray, do not forsake me, O God, till I declare your power
to the next generation, your might to all who are to come." The
psalmist Asaph declares, "We will not hide them [teachings]
from their children; we will tell the next generation the praise-
worthy deeds of the lord, his power, and the wonders he has
done." (Psalm 78:4) Psalm 102:18 says, "Let this be written for
a future generation, that a people not yet created may praise the
Lord."

Great men and women of the faith were committed to passing
along the knowledge of God to the next generation. In Deuteronomy 11:18–21, Moses reminds Israel to pass along the words
of God to their children: "Fix these words of mine in your hearts

and minds; tie them as symbols on your hands and bind them on your foreheads. Teach them to your children, talking about them when you sit at home and when you walk along the road, when you lie down and when you get up. Write them on the door-frames of your houses and on your gates, so that your days and the days of your children may be many in the land that the lord swore to give your forefathers, as many as the days that the heavens are above the earth."

It is the responsibility of the first generation to pass along the ways of the Lord and the knowledge of him to the second generation. This is most important—more than passing along history, tradition, trivia, or understanding of administrative systems and organizational structure—that the first generation passes along *the knowledge of God!* It is the responsibility of the second generation to obey and pursue the Lord instead of the blessings passed on to them. The first generation of Israelites who entered the Promised Land had to fight for the privilege of receiving the blessings. The second generation was born in blessings. Perhaps this is actually not a great blessing at all, to be born in blessing.

NEW PHARISEES AND INSTITUTIONALIZATION

It seems that every revival, awakening, renewal, movement of God goes through the three stages. The last stage, the *ashes* stage, marks the death of the move of God. Some suggest that God departed from the movement. I suggest the people departed from God. The Bible is clear: if we forsake the Lord and his ways, we will reap death and curses in almost every single facet of life.

(Deuteronomy 29:24–29) Life does not work without the Spirit of God present in a real and active way in all areas of our lives.

According to 2,000-plus years of church history, institutionalization is inevitable. The very structures and programs built to sustain, maintain, and captain a fresh move of God's Spirit end up taking over. Somewhere, even imperceptibly, structure gains the lead—structure drops down into the driver's seat and the Holy Spirit is shoved over into the co-pilot seat. Soon, the structure demands more and more time, resources and provision as it increases, eventually snuffing out the Spirit's fire. Eventually, the structure exists completely apart from the aid of the Holy Spirit. Most frightful is this: leaders usually never see it coming. One day the revival has become a funeral, and yet the leaders are still dancing. Leaders of a once-fresh move of God that has turned to a dead structure are often of the New Pharisee version. In fact, it is in *the institution* where the New Pharisee can selfishly indulge the most.

New Pharisees in places of spiritual leadership have a hard time realizing the institution is dead. In fact, they probably do not even recognize that the organization they oversee has institutionalized at all. Institutionalism is marked by a veneration of particular founding leaders and/or organizations, though no longer following the values, integrity, and direction of those founders.

...it is in *the institution* where the New Pharisee can selfishly indulge the most.

Perhaps you are a New Pharisee who is in place of leadership over an institutionalized organization that once burned with the first-love flames of devotion to Christ. You can be a conduit for a return to that same dynamic, if you would simply chose Christ and obedience to his word in your life. Nicodemus was a Pharisee who made this brave choice. I am sure he would tell you he never regretted that decision.

Bringing this closer to home, we should ask ourselves if we have become institutionalized. A few years ago, the youth of many nations began repeating an almost-forgotten phrase: "What would Jesus do?" Taken from one of the most popular Christian books ever written, *In His Steps* by Charles Sheldon, the question remains as timely as ever. Reverend Henry Maxwell was pastor of the fictitious First Church of Raymond. After a most unusual and heart-rending plea from a strange visitor, the congregation of First Church was cut to the quick—they realized they were not living according to the same standards as their founder, savior, and so-called Lord.

The following Sunday, Pastor Maxwell offered them this challenge:

> At the close of the service, I want all those members who are willing to join such a company to remain and we will talk over the details of the plan. Our motto will be, "What would Jesus do?" Our aim will be to act just as He would if He was in our places, regardless of immediate results. In other words, we propose to follow Jesus' steps as closely and as literally as we believe he taught his disciples to do. And those who volunteer to do this will pledge themselves for an entire year, beginning with today, so to act.[5]

If you read the rest of the story, you will discover that many people in First Church took on this challenge. Their lives changed drastically. They suffered persecution and mockery. Some of them lost high-paying jobs and others lost reputations with people in their field. But these same people gained a love, peace, and eternal revelation that, to them, were worth far more than gold and silver, fame, and glory. Not only this, but they went out into their town and into their community and made a difference. People not only were born into the kingdom of God, but the sin and bondage in their lives was removed. Many were set free!

As individuals broke free from institutionalization, the institution itself caught fire and a new flame of passion and compassion blazed through First Church and eventually into the entire town of Raymond. *This is revival!* If a flame flickers within the four walls, yet never breaks into the community, and sets fire to the people outside the church, I think both Finney and Maxwell would say, "Sorry, but this is no revival. Not yet, anyway."

Henri Nouwen made this observation about moving out of the four walls of our churches:

> Those who are marginal in the world are central in the Church, and that is how it is supposed to be! Thus, we are called as members of the Church to keep going to the margins of our society. The homeless, the starving, parentless children, people with AIDS, our emotionally disturbed brothers and sisters— they require our first attention…We can trust that when we reach out with all our energy to the margins of our society we will discover that petty disagreements, fruitless debates, and paralyzing rivalries will recede and gradually vanish. The church will

always be renewed when our attention shifts from ourselves to those who need our care.[6]

A true revival will change the people of God, and then result in the people of God setting free a lost and dying world. The church will grow exponentially with almost no effort—clothed with humility and Christ-likeness, and delightfully free of the pride and self-righteous exclusivism of the New Pharisee!

As Finney points out, a revival of white-hot love for God and our fellow man must include regular instances of commitments and recommitments to follow Jesus' example:

> Awakening collapses when Christians won't practice self-denial. When people experience revival and begin to grow fat on it, they run off to indulge themselves, the revival will soon end. Unless they sympathize with the Son of God, who gave up everything to save sinners, and unless they are willing to surrender luxuries and commit themselves to the job, they shouldn't bother to expect God to pour out his Spirit on them. Self-indulgence is one of the primary causes of individuals falling away. Beware when you first find an inclination creeping in to shrink from self-denial and give into one gratification after another. It is Satan's device to bait you away from the work of God, making you dull and gross, lazy, fearful, useless and sensual, and to drive away the Spirit and destroy revival.[7]

Finney is perhaps the most widely respected revivalist of the modern age for the simple fact that he preached repentance of sins and a return to loving and obeying God. There was no manipulation or control tactics with Finney—other than the exhortation to repent of sins. If preaching with convincing and persuasive arguments is considered manipulation, then Jesus, the disciples, and Paul are guilty of manipulation as well. God

works through human instruments. To be sure, the Old Testa
ment prophets preached and prophesied with conviction and
persuasion, just as Finney did. I see no difference. I believe we
must recapture much of what Finney thought and did in our
generation if there is any eternal hope for this next century.

NOBLE REVIVALS ONLY, PLEASE!

It must be pointed out that many revivals today that include
freakish signs and wonders are many times revealed to be nothing more than shenanigans of human design. Other revivals are
simply human attempts to work up a crowd and get them to
respond emotionally without any kind of conviction regarding
spiritual truth. And then there are the revivals that more resemble the kinds of things the Pharisees were after by way of stern
admonitions to take up various forms of legalism. On the more
honorable side, there have been many manifestations of the
miraculous and supernatural.

The only revival the Bible requires is that of relationship with
God and others. A revival that reunites us with our Father, and
our families—this is the revival that is noble. All we need in this
or any other day is a *noble* revival. Is that to say that other revivals are less noble? Yes! Of course! If we could return to our first
love, there is no telling what God might accomplish in us and
through us. Most importantly, a revival of our first love with
God is the fulfillment of our purpose for being created in the
first place.

As men and women, our identity has been tampered with
since the moment of our birth. We think our worth is wrapped

up in what we produce. But God would say to you, to man or woman of God, that your worth is wrapped up in this one fact: that he loves you! He could have created you with no limbs and no ability to produce anything, and he would love you and accept you no less! He cares *not* what you produce or what you accomplish! He cares *not at all!* Perhaps you have a pet dog, or cat. Or perhaps you have a favorite model, artistic creation, or possession. Do you care whether your creation can produce something for you? No! You care simply because you created it! You love that which you created, not because of what it will produce for you, but because *you created* it.

Of course, God wants us to obey out of a love relationship with him. And, obedience will result in producing certain results, tangible and sometimes intangible. God will judge what we do, to be sure, but only as it is directly related to how much we love him! (Matthew 7:21–24)

10

Breaking Old Wineskins

I saved this chapter for last for many reasons; the main reason is that I think practical strategies and structures regarding church and ministry work are doomed for failure if the core issues of the heart are not dealt with *on the front end*. Of course, we have a tendency in the west in particular to be pragmatists. We aren't as concerned with interior growth of the human spirit as much as we are with exterior growth of church structures, strategies, buildings, and programs.

We aren't as concerned with interior growth of the human spirit as much as we are with exterior growth of church structures...

Some people think programs are bad. They are not. Programs are as Spirit-led and anointed as the people that oversee them. I propose that programs and structures never have been the major problem with the church today or yesterday. The major problem has to do with the last nine chapters of this book. The major problem with church structure is the *people that run them!*

I am not saying that some programs are not invalid, unjust, or simply sinful and twisted. But I *am* saying that hearts rightly related to God will obey the values God has burned within their souls—and change those programs that need changing. Perhaps some programs must be eliminated altogether. Perhaps certain structures are no longer up to date and must be thrown out or revamped. Perhaps entirely new structures and concepts must be birthed *out of the biblical values.*

But the point is structure is subservient to those who are in leadership. A leader can't blame a program he or she has authority and ability to alter. Leaders over old structures or programs fail to change them because, at the end of the day, they are not truly willing to change them. If it takes pioneering a whole new work of God, it is up to the pioneers to move out, obey God, and build the proper structures and programs. Structures and programs are needed. New wineskins are always necessary. You cannot read the New Testament and come away saying the apostles avoided structure and programs because they used structure and programs. (Acts 2:42–47; 4:35; 6:1–7; 14:23; 1 Corinthians 12:28; 2 Corinthians 8:1–24; 16:1–4; 16:16; 1 Timothy 5:9–16)

Greg Laurie says, "I'm more interested in the heart of the church, the passion of its people, the inner fire that changes things in spite of size, programs, or numbers. Too many of us are caught up in the outside stuff—focusing on numbers, building programs, and the latest ways to attract new members. And in the process, we've lost sight of our first love. We've lost our light, our burning fire, to see people turn to Christ."[1]

Many today realize that the church is in need of some new wineskins. The cries for deconstruction and revolution are evident across the board in Christian circles and denominations. I think this cry is valid. I think we are most definitely at a place and time where *new wine* is available but is in serious need of *new wineskins* to hold it.

Certain principles must be adhered to if a person or church desires to be biblically correct. Any serious leader must read Howard A. Snyder's timeless book *The Problem of Wineskins: Church Structure in a Technological Age*. In it, Snyder points out the biblical non-negotiables in terms of creating new wineskins: "The church as the community of God's people should be structured on spiritual gifts of leadership and on some form of large-group and small-group gatherings. Beyond this, the church should take care to distinguish between its essential self and all parachurch structures so that it does not become culture-bound, and so that, conversely, in periods of upheaval the wine is not thrown out with the wineskins."[2]

In Acts 2:42–47, we see this general structure in the early church (as fluid, adaptable, and relevant as it was and forever should be) as the apostles began to preach and teach after Pentecost:

They devoted themselves to the apostles' teaching and to the fellowship [Greek, *koinonia*], to the breaking of bread and to prayer. Everyone was filled with awe, and many wonders and miraculous signs were done by the apostles. All the believers were together and had everything in common. Selling their possessions and goods, they gave to anyone as he had need. Every day they continued to meet together in the temple courts. They broke bread in their homes and ate together with glad and sincere hearts, praising God and enjoying the favor of all the people. And the Lord added to their number daily those who were being saved.

They met in the temple courts in large groups. They met in their homes as many small groups. They probably had some forms of parachurch structures already in operation, primarily those that help care for the poor and needy. (Para-church means coming alongside the church to help assist the church with specialized needs that required particular structure to administrate them successfully.) They experienced dynamic *koinonia*.

SMALL GROUPS

Every day the early church met in homes for prayer, fellowship, and eating together. There is nothing quite like a meal to bring an intimate element into a gathering. Almost every time human beings get together, food is present. People even eat at funerals. Exceptions of course, would be prayer meetings and more formal large group gatherings. The early Christians didn't want to eat by themselves. They wanted the fellowship of other believers.

Pastor Rob Bell shares in *Velvet Elvis,* "To be part of the [first century] church was to join a countercultural society that was partnering with God to create a new kind of culture, right under the nose of the Caesars. These Christians made sure everybody in their midst had enough to eat. They made sure everybody was able to pay his bills. They made sure there was enough to go around. The resurrection for them was not an abstract spiritual concept; it was a concrete social and economic reality."[3]

Food or no food, the group dynamics that are unique to small groups have a very necessary function. Group discussion is best when in a small group. When Christians speak out what they believe, they really come to own their faith personally. If they are confused or have questions, these questions are best answered in small groups. In fact, Jesus and the twelve were a small group. Jesus used the small group dynamic for discipling the apostles. Small groups are also useful for facilitating praying for each other, listening to each other, and counseling each other.

In *The Signature of Jesus,* Brennan Manning states, "Gathered in the name of Jesus, the community empowers us to incarnate in our lives what we believe in our hearts and proclaim with our lips…We need a group of people around us who support and understand us, the base community. Even Jesus needed this: He called them, 'The Twelve,' the first Christian community. We need perspective on the present, so we pray together; we need accountability, so we share our lives with each other; we need a vision of the future, so we dream together."[4]

A variety of small groups exists in scripture. Jesus and the twelve were more of an accountability/mentoring group, whereas in Acts 2:42–47, the group was mainly used as a fel-

lowship and pastoral care structure. No church community can
hope to care for and disciple others adequately outside of the
small group. It is amazing that many ministers today have considerable experience in all aspects of ministry except small
groups. For some reason, small groups are not always a priority
in formal ministry training. However, if we hope to build new
wineskins that hold new wine, we must use the small group as
the central tool in caring for and discipling others as they did in
the early church.

**No church community can hope to care for
and disciple others adequately outside of the
small group.**

LARGE GROUP

In the early church, the large group was a gathering of the
local church community in the city. There was a desire to come
together in the temple courts for teaching, preaching, corporate
worship, and encouragement. When Christians gather, there is
an unspoken dynamic of faith and excitement. Large group
gatherings provide opportunities to give and receive from the
greater church body. Hearing from gifted teachers and preachers is best accomplished in a large gathering. Vital reports of
praise, as well as needs for prayers for the city church were
announced in the large gathering.

The Spirit also provides great encouragement and exhortation
in the large gathering. The large group gathering of Israel under

the direction of Nehemiah and Ezra, just after the completion of the rebuilt walls of Jerusalem, was useful for the Spirits' conviction and renewal. Ezra read from the Word of God all day long, until the spirit came with conviction. Israel repented and was changed as a result. (Nehemiah 7–10) Also, the large group gathering is the best environment for music and worship. Members with musical gifts are able to use their talents to edify the body in the large group context.

KOINONIA

Koinonia is the Greek word for fellowship. Unfortunately, like a lot of English words, fellowship is a rather shallow translation for *koinonia*. *Koinonia* is better defined as deep fellowship with other people, and the very real and felt presence of the Holy Spirit. When this dynamic is present in a room of Christians, it is very intoxicating. I know people who actually became addicted to true *koinonia* to the point of idolatry. Many will come to a *koinonia*-filled church, not for God himself, but for the fantastic feeling of God's loving presence in people's hearts and minds. It is probably a matter of discipleship that we turn people's hearts and attention always on the Lord himself and his love for us. Nevertheless, God commands us to love one another. Many will be drawn to us because of his presence. If we remain faithful, many of these will eventually come to know God himself because of our love for each other.

The archaic structures and old wineskins that prevent *koinonia* should be eliminated. In terms of building structure, it really first requires that those who would build that structure be released from all that would keep the New Pharisee alive within. Leaders must pave the way in humility, vulnerability, and compassion if they hope to experience *koinonia*. If not, might as well leave the old wineskins intact—new wineskins are irrelevant without wine. Leaders who live in *koinonia* will facilitate that same *koinonia* for others, and will tweak structure until it properly embraces and enhances *koinonia*. Pastors and apostolic leaders must recognize that developing intimate fellowship among their congregations is their *a priori* (supreme) responsibility.

PARA-CHURCH ORGANIZATIONS

Some say if the church did its job, there would be no need for parachurch organizations. I think the opposite is true. I think when the church is doing its job, parachurch organizations are created to deal with specialized needs. If the question is simply a matter of a church housing the organization under its administrative umbrella, we must realize that in New Testament times, there was no possibility of a church being administratively advanced enough in its structure in order to be able to keep things under its direct control.

Think of many saints who sit in the pew for years, and perhaps God has called them to serve the poor, young, old, imprisoned, lost, unreached, bed-ridden, starving, and abused. They may initially minister within the local church structure, but as God blesses and blossoms their ministry, the growth may necessitate that these folks leave their vocation and give themselves part-time or full-time for the continuation of the ministry. That is what I think the goal of every church should be. Why do we always have to keep people within the four walls of our church structures administratively? Eventually, this desire to keep things in house will stunt the growth of something that could become a very influential ministry in the community and even in the world.

Some churches are able to pay someone to do the parachurch ministry in house. If that is the Spirit's direction, wonderful. But, some churches many times become competitive with the kingdom of God. They do not want a *pew sitter* to be raised up by the Lord and do a great work for God because of selfish reasons. New Pharisees are not excited when God raises someone out of their midst to do something great. Rather, they are threatened. Foolish thinking!

LEADERS MUST LEAD THOSE WHO FOLLOW

To those of us who currently attend or pastor a mega-church, I would urge you to take note of this fact: community is not merely a mythological or mystical idea, but a concrete objective reality. Community exists where there is sharing, feeling, caring, loving, listening, hugging, praying, grieving, comforting, counseling, giving, forgiving, correcting, and encouraging. In a mega-church model, these essential components of true community will be found, for the most part, within a small group context rather than a large corporate service. (I say model because we have chosen this method of doing church, not so much because it is *the* model that the Holy Spirit has anointed, but more because it is based on the kinds of organizational models that contemporary western men and women know how to do best.) Leaders of mega-churches must come to grips with this fact and redirect, or even reorganize their strategies and structures to accommodate small groups as central tools for discipleship, care, counsel, and comfort.

Gordon MacDonald expressed some of his shocking revelations regarding his own church struggles as he began meetings with a small group of disgruntled church members in his eye-opening book *Who Stole My Church?*:

> *What in the world is happening here?* I asked myself. It was as if we were at a costume party where, at the stroke of midnight, everyone had to remove their disguises. People were exposing their broken hearts and sharing the darker parts of their own private stories for the first time. Faces, usually smiling and projecting confidence, were now marked with deep pain and struggle. Burdens of worry, grief, confusion, and regret, never before mentioned, were being placed, as it were, right on the table. No one in the room was more shaken at these disclosures than I was. I'd been preaching to these people week after week and didn't have the slightest idea that some of these things were going on in their hearts.[5]

We must no longer erroneously suppose that any real sense of community can be attained through the large corporate gatherings alone. The corporate service/gathering is best suited for a weekly rallying point, a celebration of all that God is doing in the midst of the people of God throughout the week. The large corporate service is where preaching, worship, and spiritual vision casting are best accomplished. Leaders of mega-churches must understand that small group ministry will not thrive in their churches until they themselves come to embrace small group values such as mentoring, one-on-one discipleship, evangelism, community, and *koinonia*.

> **We must no longer erroneously suppose that any real sense of community can be attained through the large corporate gatherings alone.**

In essence, the corporate service is validated to the extent that community is experienced among the body throughout the week in smaller groups. Small groups must be developed from a heart of passion and compassion.

If leaders attempt to install small groups into their church solely for gaining more attendees, it is better to have no groups at all. There are plenty of case studies that validate this point—that small groups will not become the primary source of community and individual discipleship unless the leadership embraces small groups as such and has firsthand experience not only in facilitating small groups, but installing qualified and equipped men and women who are called to lead such groups.

Leaders who lack experience in leading, or even taking part in small groups should take heart: your congregants most likely have less experience than you do! You can all follow the Spirit together and learn together under the Spirit's tutelage. In fact, this is the best place you can possibly be as a leader, fully dependant on God to come through in response to your obedience and trust, and careful adherence to what you have found in the Bible in terms of commands for church life and oversight.

There are numerous books coming out on small groups. Various churches are having great success with small groups, while others struggle. Keep in mind that most visitors tend to enjoy coming to events and activities before they will feel comfortable in an intimate small group. I would include women's groups, men's groups, youth groups, and children's groups in my definition of small groups. The cell, most widely known for being a group that grows in numbers as well as community, is not the best tool for evangelism perhaps. The cell, by definition, has to grow both in numbers and in maturity for it to be an actual cell. Accountability groups, for example, are not intended to reach new people or lost people. Most often, accountability groups produce intimacy and vulnerability with Christians who are developing strong relationships with each other—heading towards the critical mass known as *koinonia*.

Affinity groups, while possibly being effective in reaching unchurched people, have a difficult time integrating those people into the church ministry. For example, an affinity group might be a church softball team where half of the players are not Christians or from your church. You may or may not find any of them actually coming to your church or even being ministered to other than just building friendships. This in itself has merit and great possibilities as long as the church understands that an affinity group cannot replace the function of a cell, or an accountability group. The affinity group could also include certain committees or leadership teams. In those cases, strong bonds can be built relationally, as well as equipping one another for leadership and maturity.

Age-level groups are extremely effective, especially in such age-segregated cultures, for developing a wide variety of ministries and groups (affinity, cell, accountability, age-level) that can all synergize together to build a vibrant ministry of evangelism and discipleship.

WHAT NEW WINESKINS?

I am tempted to provide numerous models of new wineskins in detail, but I think God would reserve that for another book. When we recapture the right heart for ministry, we will automatically capture the right models. The Holy Spirit is creative and is able to provide some fabulous ideas to the simple greenhorn who has no idea what to do in ministry. I do not mean to say that training and equipping is not necessary. Neither do I mean to imply that people do not need advisement on what kinds of wineskins to build. But I still say the Holy Spirit may rather show you a new idea.

David was a youth, but he had already beaten the bear and the lion when he met Goliath head-to-head. Saul and his men had experience and maturity and I am sure they were competent leaders, but they were missing one thing: child-like faith. In the final analysis, perhaps this is the only thing that is really needed.

Gone must be the days of human marketing techniques and technology as the *primary energy and power* source for the sustaining and advancing of the kingdom of God in any and every local community. It is time to utilize these tools, not as substitute for *the primary power,* but as supplemental and subservient to The Primary Power: the Holy Spirit!

Howard Snyder says, "The church must be a genuine community in which wholeness of life grows out of praise to God and fellowship with all men in Christ, without resort to demeaning techniques. The church must grow because of genuine spiritual magnetism, not by religious technology or contentless experience." He goes further, "They [today's followers] must learn to wait upon the Lord, to be sensitive to his leadings and to depend less and less on the arm of flesh."[6]

Robert Girard said, "Anything in the church program that cannot be maintained without constant pastoral pressure on the people to be involved should be allowed to die a sure and natural death."[7] I would add that these dying things might not be bad things. In fact, they may be essential. Perhaps the people in the body are of such a spiritual state that what should flow out naturally in the Spirit's power is over-burdening them in the flesh. The answer, in that case, is not necessarily to cease doing these things permanently, but to suspend them temporarily until the people are on a healthy road to renewal and restoration with the Lord.

GOD'S CALLING

As long as the new wineskin stays within the biblical principles of church—large groups, small groups, parachurch, discipleship, and dynamic *koinonia*—I think there should be freedom to be culturally relevant. God's idea was and is the church! We must think of the local church as a body. The new wineskins will allow the body to build itself up in love.

Jesus promised in Matthew 10:41, "Anyone who receives a prophet because he is a prophet will receive a prophet's reward, and anyone who receives a righteous man because he is a righteous man will receive a righteous man's reward." If you and I bless and serve Mother Theresa or Billy Graham, we will receive the same reward. Why? Because ultimately, no one can boast of any reward other than Christ himself. Can Billy Graham rightly claim sole responsibility for all the souls that have come to Christ through his preaching? What about those who pray, or those who organize behind the scenes? What about the godly mothers, fathers, and siblings who have prayed for that lost one for years? What about others who planted seeds? Paul said, "I planted the seed, Apollos watered it, but God made it grow. So neither he who plants nor he who waters is anything, but only God, who makes things grow." (1 Corinthians 3:6–7)

...get on your knees and repent of such a wicked heart as to allow any amount of competition and selfish ambition in your soul!

Jealousy and envy are shortsighted for the person who claims to believe in heaven, because when they get to heaven, they will be embarrassed to realize their competitive acts and thoughts may have hindered others from being great in the kingdom. It will also result in being ashamed eternally. If you really believe that there is a heaven and a just God, get on your knees and

repent of such a wicked heart as to allow any amount of competition and selfish ambition in your soul!

Surely, the day will come when you cry out in shame at the
prospect that you may have stolen people away from eternal life
forever, simply because you were jealous of another's successful
ministry!

In addition to this, gaining recognition and acclaim is the
stuff of Pharisees, not of Christians. Because Pharisees have
already received their reward in full, there will be no eternal
reward for them. If we are to embrace the new wineskins, which
must have biblical foundations, we must let go of the desires
inside us that would tear down the body, and not build it up. The
New Pharisee loves the praise of men. The Christian is full of
joy when her works go unnoticed and she remains unknown, for
great is her reward in heaven!

...gaining recognition and acclaim is the stuff of Pharisees, not of Christians.

Truly, those famous leaders who are praised in Christendom
today are not necessarily praised in the same way by the hosts
of heaven. But I believe the kindness of a meek widow may
gain more praise from the universe of heavenly beings. In fact,
leadership is simply a gift. God is no more impressed with a
great leader than with a great follower. I think he's more
impressed with a great follower. I think the least *actually will
be* the greatest!

The New Pharisee in you and me will oppose us. Dethrone the New Pharisee now! Let not eternal embarrassment be your only future prospect.

LAST NIGHT I WENT TO A BOWLING ALLEY...

The first hour, I was looking down on every sinner who was carousing and drinking. I felt great dislike rising up inside me for many of them. Meanwhile, I needed to finish my game, and get home to my book and write more on *The New Pharisee*. And as I struggled to knock down thirty pins in the first five frames, it hit me: these sinners that I am not enjoying are the reason Christ died. He loves them! He loves them so much! How much? This much: I'm holding out my arms in shape of a cross; you've seen this example before, right?

Jesus feels right at home in the presence of sinners.

That's how much Jesus loves sinners. He didn't ignore them as I did. He loved them and spent time with them. In fact, he preferred being in their presence to the presence of the Pharisees. Jesus feels right at home in the presence of sinners. Sinners always liked Jesus. He was their friend. Remember when you were a sinner? Aren't you glad Jesus didn't avoid you? We all want people to see us for what we really are on the inside. We fear people judging us by outward appearances. As humans, wise people learn that outward appearances are a sham and folly. The wise one learns that the spirit is altogether separate from the façade of our temporary human likeness.

So I was burdened with the cruelty of my own heart as I held that old, cold, black sphere in my hand.

And then a miracle happened! Right before my eyes, these sinners became the most loveable people! I couldn't take my eyes off of them. I stared at them, not in human terms, but as people whom God loved. I felt a warmness and compassion well up inside. Like *The Grinch,* my heart became two sizes too big right there! And you know what? I could hardly hold back myself from doing something about it.

When you love, you cannot help but do something about it! This is revival as it works out in me. When I walk in personal revival, I find I must do something because of the love overflowing inside of me, love that replaced the coldness and hatred of my own wicked heart.

As the evening wore on, I then managed to offer half smiles of congratulations when one of these sinners bowled a strike. Funny, they didn't seem like sinners anymore, just people. We're all sinners. And apart from Christ, I would be much worse than most of them. I liked it there, and I think I'll go back again.

When the church gets back to this dynamic, I think we won't need to worry about getting people into our churches. They will flock in by the droves. The number of new converts in our nation would probably quadruple in the first year alone.

Epilogue

Nicodemus heard the news: Jesus of Nazareth was arrested last night.

After all the wonderful things Jesus did, this is what he got. This is the way his countrymen showed their appreciation. On this day, the crowd would be incensed beyond all rationality by the lies and deception of the Jewish elders and Sanhedrin. On this day, Nicodemus would observe the kangaroo court, the completely unjust treatment of Jesus, and then the terrible decision to crucify him. On this day, the Roman soldiers would watch a man who claimed to be God being condemned to die by his own people, and they would despise him, spit upon him, mock him, and beat him senseless...and nail him to a beastly block of wood.

Had this been a few years earlier, Nicodemus would not have comprehended it. But for some reason, he now saw things differently. He had probably read in Isaiah 53:3–5, "He was despised and rejected by men, a man of sorrows, and familiar with suffering. Like one from whom men hide their faces he was despised, and we esteemed him not. Surely, he took upon our infirmities and carried our sorrows, yet we considered him stricken by God, smitten by him, and afflicted. But he was pierced for our transgressions, he was crushed for our iniquities; the punishment that brought us peace was upon him, and by his wounds we are healed."

Before Nicodemus met Jesus, he looked for a victorious Roman conqueror who would establish a throne of world peace and domination and once again set the Jews in power over the people of the earth. But now, Nicodemus knew the *true* Messiah could not really be those things—not yet. Now, he realized that the greatest domination happens *from within* men and women. Now he could comprehend the truth that the kingdom of God is not here, or there, but within the hearts of those who love God and obey God. Now Nicodemus could see that the terrible things being done to Jesus of Nazareth were also very necessary. This death of the perfect spotless lamb—God's own Son—was actually the ultimate victory. God had been setting it up all the time.

Nicodemus perhaps followed the crowd from a distance as he watched Jesus being led up to Golgotha. He watched Jesus being tied to the cross, and crucified between two thieves. He watched the soldiers cast lots to trade the clothes. He listened as Jesus breathed his last breath and cried out, "It is finished!" Then Jesus dropped his head. It was truly finished. He was dead. God died? Nicodemus peered across the crowd, looking for his disciples and relatives. Some were at the foot of the cross weeping. Most of the disciples were nowhere to be found. Why didn't they stick around?

The next day, Joseph of Arimathea asked Pilate if he could have the body of Jesus so that he could embalm and bury him. Joseph was a disciple of Jesus, but secretly because he feared the Jews. (John 19:38) Pilate granted his request. Nicodemus heard about this and instinctively volunteered to help Joseph with the burial. The old Pharisee in Nicodemus was long gone. He may have been a Pharisee outwardly, but just like Joseph of Arimathea, he too had been changed on the inside. They were both ruling members of the Jewish leaders. Joseph himself was a rich member of the Sanhedrin, and openly disapproved of Jesus' condemnation. (Luke 23:51) Pharisees on the outside, true believers on the inside. Now they had an opportunity to be more public about their faith.

Jesus' closest followers may have deserted him, but not Joseph and Nicodemus. They came to the tomb, and they laid the body of Jesus there. Nicodemus suddenly felt a surge of emotion. He could not contain his passion. He had purchased enough embalming material for a royal burial, and at great cost to himself. He did not see it as a cost; he saw this as a privilege! He and Joseph prepared the body in a mixture of aloes and myrrh, with linen strips wrapped around the body.

What went through Nicodemus' mind at this moment? How could he remain convinced that Jesus was the Son of God, and yet see now his dead body lying before him? Of course he was heartbroken, but maybe he was also hopeful. Nicodemus spent a huge amount on this burial. Both he and Joseph were taking a considerable risk. What would their fellow elders say about them giving this condemned man a royal Jewish burial?

Perhaps deep down, Nicodemus knew something was not right with this picture. Perhaps Nicodemus still believed that Jesus would live again. Regardless, they both knew that Jesus was watching them from above. They wanted to please their new Lord and King. If only they could have known what was about to happen in a few days! Nicodemus buried the body of Jesus on Saturday. Sunday, Nicodemus heard the news from Mary and the disciples: Jesus is risen from the dead! Halleluiah!

Most probably, Nicodemus was one of the 500 believers who watched Jesus ascend into the clouds. And most certainly, Nicodemus was a tremendous witness for Christ for the rest of his life. For what man would not be a bold witness who personally embalmed a dead body, and then saw that body raised to life? Not only this, he and 500 others watched Jesus ascend into heaven! If that doesn't make a true revived believer out of you, nothing will.

Now how about you? Perhaps you are a hypocrite—a genuine Pharisee, and if you were one of the Pharisees at the time of Christ, you too would have been angry with Jesus. Maybe you would have hated him. It doesn't really matter. What matters is that you want to change. I have a feeling Nicodemus did not like Jesus at first either. Jesus told us the truth—about God and about ourselves. People get killed often for such things. Nicodemus wanted to change. He was willing to face the music. He was willing to count the cost. He was willing to exchange the

temporary pleasures of this life for eternal pleasures forever-
more. More than this, he wanted to love God. He wanted to
please his Creator.

Nicodemus removed the Pharisee from within himself. Take
his example as encouragement for you today. God loves you!
All of us have gone astray from his intent and purpose for us.
There is always hope. Jesus Christ is that hope. Nicodemus
found this hope, and embraced him *with all his heart, soul,
mind, and strength.* Now you can, too.

A suggested prayer:

Prayer of Repentance for the New Pharisee

Dear Lord,

*We confess to you that our hearts have not been consumed
with you. We confess that sometimes we honor you with our lips
while our hearts are far from you. Forgive us for the times we
have not sought your face, but the things of this world. Cleanse
us from our impure motives. Turn us from evil ways of self-promotion, selfish ambition, fearing man, and manipulating situations for our own welfare—while calling it your will. Oh, God!
Turn our eyes to see the kingdom of heaven. Oh, God! Shine
your light into the darkness of our souls and send the filth and
infection away. We wish to be pure. We wish to promote only you
and your glory. Let us join as the body of Christ and build one
another up in the faith, instead of tearing down one another,
thinking we will better ourselves. We have been deceived into
thinking that putting others down lifts us up. But Lord, right
now in the light of the truth of your Word and presence, we see
that we find our life when we lose it. And now we see, Lord, that*

we bless ourselves when we meet the needs of others. God, we are beginning to understand that we promote ourselves only by promoting others ahead of us. We believe that you will reward those who truly yearn to be the least. Make it so in us, Father! AMEN.

Notes

PROLOGUE

1. Daniel Elton Harmon, *"What Ever Happened To Blondin?" Blithering Antiquity* 1, no. 2 (Feb 2003).

2. Matthew 16:24

3. Matthew 16:6

CHAPTER 1

1. "Most religious groups in USA have lost ground, survey finds," USA Today, McLean, VA, **Mar 9, 2009**.

2. *"The Year's Most Intriguing Findings **from Barna Research Studies,"** George Barna Research Group, Ventura, CA, **Dec 12, 2000.**

3. *The NIV Study Bible* (Grand Rapids: The Zondervan Corporation, 1985), 1496.

4. The Works of Josephus, The Antiquities of the Jews, Book 13, Chapter 10:5

5.———Acts 10:17

6. *The NIV Study Bible* (Grand Rapids: The Zondervan Corporation, 1985), 1496.

7. Matthew 23:1-39

8. *The NIV Study Bible* (Grand Rapids: The Zondervan Corporation, 1985), 1476.

9. The Works of Josephus, The Antiquity of the Jews, Book 18, Chapter 1:3

CHAPTER 2

1. John 8:39

2. David Kinnaman and The Barna Group, *UnChristian* (Grand Rapids: Baker Books, 2007), 26-28.

3. Melody Green & David Hazard, *No Compromise: The Life Story of Keith Green* (Eugene: Harvest House Publishers, 1989), 193.

4. John Darby, *Synopsis of the New Testament,* ch. 3.

5. C. S. Lewis, *Mere Christianity* (New York: Harper Collins Publishers, 2001), 202.

6. Charles Swindoll, *Moses: A Man of Selfless Dedication* (Nashville: Word Pub., 1999), 238.

7. Dietrich Bohnhoeffer, *The Cost of Discipleship* (New York: Macmillan SCM Press, 1959), 51.

8. Thomas Merton, *Passion For Peace* (New York: Crossroad Publishing, 1995), 70.

9. Walter A. Henrichsen, *Disciples Are Made—Not Born* (Wheaton, Illinois: SP Pub., 1974), 21.

CHAPTER 3

1. *Merriam-Webster's Collegiate Dictionary*, 11th ed. (Springfield, Massachusetts: Merriam Webster Inc., 2003).

2. C. S. Lewis, *Mere Christianity* (New York: Harper Collins Pub., 2000), 208

3. "The New Testament seems to combine the Old Testament concept of the godless rebel and the Attic Greek *hypokrisis* stage-playing or acting. The Greek idea of play-acting seems paramount in Matthew 6:2, 5, and 16, where Jesus warns against religious performance to impress men (vv. 5, 16, 18 cf.). Hypocrites make an outward show of religion, whether in giving alms, praying, or fasting. The English concept of hypocrisy as failing to practice what one preaches is rarely found (Matt 23:3)." Greg W. Parsons, *Baker's Evangelical Dictionary of Biblical Theology* (Grand Rapids: Baker Book House, 1996).

4. Watchman Nee, *Sit, Walk, Stand* (Bombay: Gospel Literature Service, 1957)

5. Matthew 12:1

6. "But he answered and said, 'It is written, Man shall not live by bread alone, but by every word [*rhema*] that proceeds from the mouth of God.'" Matthew 4:4

7. Charles G. Finney, *Lectures On Revival* (Minneapolis: Bethany House Pub., 1988). 142.

8. Dick Foth, *"It's Worth It!"* (lecture, National Youth For Christ Annual Convention, San Antonio, Texas, 1998).

9. *The Princess Bride,* Twentieth Century Fox, 1988

10. Otis Lockett, *"Believe the Gospel"* (lecture, New Generation Ministries Conference, Charlotte, NC, 1993).

11. Joyce Meyer, *Knowing God Intimately: Being as Close to Him as You Want to Be,* (New York: Warner Books, 2004), 45.

Chapter 4

1. Harper Lee, *To Kill a Mockingbird,* (Philadelphia: J.B. Lippencott, 1960).

2. Phillip Yancey, *The Jesus I Never Knew,* (Grand Rapids: Zondervan Pub. House, 1995), 155.

3. Charles Colson and Ellen Santilli Vaughn, *The Body: Being Light in the Darkness,* (Dallas: Thomas Nelson, 1992), 304.

4. Scotty Smith and Steven Curtis Chapman, *Speechless: Living in Awe of God's Disruptive Grace* (Grand Rapids: Zondervan Pub. House, 1999), 68.

Chapter 5

1. *Merriam-Webster's Collegiate Dictionary,* 11th ed. (Springfield, Massachusetts: Merriam-Webster Inc., 2003).

2. *Bridge Over the River Kwai* (Columbia Pictures, 1957).

Chapter 6

1. John Piper, *What Jesus Demands from the World* (Wheaton: Crossway Books, Good News Pub., 2006), 103.

2. Amy Grant, *Amy Grant,* "Mountaintop," lyrics: Brown Bannister (Waco, Texas: Myrrh Records, 1977).

3. John Fischer, *Finding God Where You Least Expect Him* (Eugene, Oregon: Harvest House Pub., 2003), 126.

4. Henri Neuwen, *Bread for the Journey: A Daybook of Wisdom and Faith* (San Francisco: Harper Pub., 1997), 60.

CHAPTER 7

1. Tony Evans, *Fire That Ignites: Living in the Power of the Holy Spirit* (Sisters, Oregon: LifeChange Books, 2003), 93.

2. Greg Laurie, *The Upside-Down Church* (Wheaton, Illinois: Tyndale House Pub., 1999), 178–179.

CHAPTER 8

1. Jeff VanVonderan, *"Authority and Spiritual Abuse"* (lecture Spiritual Abuse Conference, Crystal, Minnesota, November 10, 1995).

2. Dan Kimble, *I Like Jesus, but I Don't Like Christians* (Grand Rapids: Zondervan, 2003), ch. 7.

3. Stuart Briscoe, (lecture from National Youth For Christ Midwinter Conference, Colorado Springs, CO, 1998).

CHAPTER 9

1. Charles G. Finney, *Lectures on Revival* (Minneapolis: Bethany House Pub., 1988), 22.

2. Ibid, 15.

3. Ibid, 15–16.

4. Henry Blackaby, *Chosen to be God's Prophet* (Nashville: Thomas Nelson Pub., 2003), 54–55.

5. Charles M. Sheldon, *In His Steps* (New York: Inspirational Press, 1998), 15.

6. Henri Nouwen, *Bread For the Journey: A Daybook of Wisdom and Faith* (San Francisco: Harper Pub., 1997), 59.

7. Charles G. Finney, *Lectures on Revival* (Minneapolis: Bethany House Pub., 1988), 180.

CHAPTER 10

1. Greg Laurie, *The Upside Down Church* (Wheaton, Illinois: Tyndale House Pub., 1999), 22.

2. Howard A. Snyder, *The Problem of Wineskins: Church Structure in a Technological Age* (Downers Grove, IL: Inter-Varsity Press, 1975), 165.

3. Rob Bell, *Velvet Elvis* (Grand Rapids: Zondervan, 2005), 163–164.

4. Brennen Manning, *The Signature Of Jesus* (Sisters, Oregon: Multnomah Books, 1988), 85–86.

5. Gordon MacDonald, *Who Stole My Church?* (Nashville: Thomas Nelson Pub., 2007), 190.

6. Howard A. Snyder, *The Problem of Wineskins: Church Structure in a Technological Age* (Downers Grove, IL: Inter-Varsity Press, 1975), 189.

7. Ibid.

About the Author

 Jeff Saxton is a writer, minister and film-maker. He directed his first feature film – *Heart of the City,* which is currently being shown at several film festivals, theaters and churches (see below for movie booking and contact information). Prior to this he was a full-time youth pastor and associate pastor for over a decade in churches in Nebraska and Minnesota. He is also a member of the *Telly Awards Silver Council* and currently resides with his wife in southern Minnesota.

For more information, contact: admin@thenewpharisee.com

Other links:
www.heartofthecitythemovie.com
www.thenewpharisee.com

LaVergne, TN USA
23 February 2011
217589LV00003B/5/P